POWERFUL
Content
Connections

Nurturing Readers, Writers, and Thinkers in Grades K–3

Jennifer L. Altieri

INTERNATIONAL
Reading Association
800 BARKSDALE ROAD, PO BOX 8139
NEWARK, DE 19714-8139, USA
www.reading.org

The International Reading Association attempts, through its publications, to provide a forum for a wide spectrum of opinions on reading. This policy permits divergent viewpoints without implying the endorsement of the Association.

Executive Editor, Publications   Shannon Fortner
Acquisitions Manager   Tori Mello Bachman
Managing Editors   Christina M. Lambert and Susanne Viscarra
Editorial Associate   Wendy Logan
Creative Services/Production Manager   Anette Schuetz
Design and Composition Associate   Lisa Kochel

Cover   Design, Shelby Alessandrini; Photographs (top left) © Purestock/Thinkstock, (middle left) © Valueline/Thinkstock, (bottom left) © Fuse/Thinkstock, (right) © Purestock/Thinkstock

The publisher would appreciate notification where errors occur so that they may be corrected in subsequent printings and/or editions.

Library of Congress Cataloging-in-Publication Data

Altieri, Jennifer L.
  Powerful content connections : nurturing readers, writers, and thinkers in grades K-3 / Jennifer L. Altieri.
      pages cm
  Includes bibliographical references and index.
  ISBN 978-0-87207-085-1
  1. Language arts (Elementary)—Standards—United States. 2. Language arts (Elementary)—Curricula—United States. 3. Language arts—Correlation with content subjects. 4. Content area reading. I. Title.
  LB1576.A615754 2013
  372.6—dc23
                                    2013026784

Suggested APA Reference
Altieri, J.L. (2014). *Powerful content connections: Nurturing readers, writers, and thinkers in grades K–3*. Newark, DE: International Reading Association.

To my former colleagues at The Citadel in Charleston, South Carolina. I will always cherish the friendship and support they provided over the past 10 years.

CONTENTS

Reproducibles

ABOUT THE AUTHOR

 **Jennifer L. Altieri** is a professor at St. John's University in Queens, New York, USA. She is the author of *Literacy + Math = Creative Connections in the Elementary Classroom* (International Reading Association [IRA], 2010) and *Content Counts! Developing Disciplinary Literacy Skills, K–6* (IRA, 2011) and coauthor of *Moving Toward an Integrated Curriculum in Early Childhood Education* (National Education Association, 1996). She has also published articles in *Teaching Children Mathematics, Teaching Exceptional Children, Reading Psychology, Reading Research and Instruction*, and other professional journals.

After completing her BS in elementary education at Bowling Green State University, Ohio, USA, Jennifer moved to Houston, Texas, USA. There she taught in the Aldine and Spring Independent School Districts. She has served as a reading consultant for elementary and middle schools in the St. Louis Public and University City school districts in St. Louis, Missouri, USA, and at Port Royal Elementary in Beaufort, South Carolina, USA. In addition, Jennifer has presented ideas for linking content areas and the Common Core State Standards as part of Carolina Biological Supply Company's Educational Leadership Series at the National Science Teachers Association. She has conducted workshops at the elementary and middle school levels on a variety of literacy topics and is known for her enthusiasm and sense of humor.

Jennifer earned her MEd from the University of Houston and her PhD from Texas A&M University. Along with serving on *The Reading Teacher*'s and *Reading Horizons*' editorial boards, she recently served on IRA's 2010 Standards Committee and the Literacy Task Force created by Mayor Riley of Charleston, South Carolina.

She recently moved to Long Island, New York, USA. When she is not working or trying to find her way around the area, she enjoys traveling to warm destinations, keeping up with her son, and writing.

Author Information for Correspondence

Jennifer welcomes your questions and comments. Please feel free to contact her at jenniferaltieri@bellsouth.net.

PREFACE

I know many of us spend a lot of time thinking about what we can do to help nurture readers, writers, and thinkers to be successful in later grades, careers, and life. We spend countless hours working, and we want to see our K–3 students become literate children who grow and mature into adults ready to meet the demands of the tasks and texts they will encounter in life. This goal aligns with the purpose of the English Language Arts Common Core State Standards (ELA CCSS). My hope is that *Powerful Content Connections: Nurturing Readers, Writers, and Thinkers in Grades K–3* will help as schools implement the standards and as teachers search for specific ideas to make the standards a reality in their classrooms.

We know the ELA CCSS contain high educational expectations, yet they must be taught within the time constraints we already experience each day. That means we have to rethink what we are teaching and how we teach it. We can do that by creating powerful connections between literacy instruction and the content areas. This will enable us not only to strengthen literacy skills but also to create content-knowledgeable children. The ELA CCSS do not specify what teachers should do to meet them; rather, they articulate the end goal. As teachers, we can use our collective wisdom to determine how to get from Point A to Point B. There are many paths that can get us to Point B, but by working together we can determine the best way to travel on the journey.

This text is designed to enable K–3 teachers to take a closer look at what the ELA CCSS are expecting from our children. Chapters focus on strengthening our early learners' literacy skills while deepening their content area knowledge by providing powerful connections between the two. That is the only way we can meet the ELA CCSS, ensure that our students have strong content knowledge, and do so within the hours we get to spend with our students.

Powerful Content Connections focuses on the use of informational text because that is the type of text that most children will use throughout their lifetime, and it is the type of text both research (Duke, 2000) and the ELA CCSS encourage. That does not mean that we must eliminate narrative stories, poetry, and plays from our classrooms. In fact, some of the examples shared within the chapters include narrative text suggestions.

However, we need to ensure that our students, regardless of age, are provided with many opportunities to engage with informational text.

It is my hope that the ideas and tools included in this book will create a discussion among those in the educational community, especially those who work the closest with our early literacy learners. Through collaborating, discussing, and reflecting on the ideas shared, even greater learning can occur. Teachers know their students best, and it is expected that ideas should and will be modified as necessary as suggestions are used.

Chapter by Chapter: Let's Look at Content

The first two chapters of this text are designed to set the stage for the rest of the text. In Chapter 1, "Empowering Our Earliest Literacy Learners," we look at how and why powerful content connections must be made. We reflect on the changes we have seen in literacy learning and take a closer look at the ELA CCSS. Beginning in Chapter 1 and continuing through the book are short features called "Try It Out," which are designed to provide readers with an opportunity to engage with the ideas discussed in the text.

In Chapter 2, "The Increasing Emphasis on Materials: Teaching With High-Quality Informational Texts," readers learn about the wide variety of available printed and digital texts and the merits and shortcomings regarding the use of some text types. Along with taking a closer look at what makes a text informational, suggestions for locating and deciding which texts might be the best fit for our needs are included. The role of materials is becoming more important because we have so many texts available.

Beginning in Chapter 3, "Creating a Strong Foundation," readers will find chapter-ending activities that target the specific ELA CCSS discussed in each chapter. Some activities could have been included in more than one chapter because they can connect easily to more than one chapter topic. Do not let the chapter topic limit thinking regarding the use of the activities. If we use purposeful planning and take advantage of teachable moments, much more can be gained from the activities. After some activities I have included "Additional Suggestions," which provide more ideas for implementing the activities with children. Also, "A Look Inside One Classroom" shows readers how a K–3 teacher implemented a specific activity in a classroom.

Chapter 3 focuses on foundational skills, which compose an entire section of the ELA CCSS. Within this chapter's pages, we look at concepts of print, phonological awareness, phonics and word recognition, and fluency. Although none of these areas are new to early childhood educators, this chapter examines how the foundational skills fit within the ELA CCSS. There are important differences to note between the foundational skills expectations for K–1 and the expectations for second- and third-grade students. Although these skills are vital to creating a foundation, we cannot focus solely on them if we hope to prepare our students for all of the literacy demands they will encounter. Understanding how these skills can connect to the overall goal of creating content area connections is explained.

In Chapter 4, "Challenging Our Students With Text," we discuss one of the most controversial aspects of ELA CCSS: text complexity. Many in the education field are concerned with preparing students to work with complex text. Using challenging text conflicts with what many of us were taught to believe when selecting the appropriate difficulty level of text for children. In this chapter, we look not only at issues that create text complexity but also at how we can assess text complexity with the texts we use in our classrooms. We also address how the expectations differ for our K–1 and second- and third-grade students. Although only students in second grade and above are expected to be able to independently read complex texts, we must begin preparation for complex text before that grade level. Our kindergartners and first-grade students must be introduced to complex text, and this chapter provides suggestions for doing that.

Vocabulary development is a skill we use our entire life. As adults, we must constantly be able to learn new words in order to understand informational text related to different topics we encounter. Therefore, there is an entire chapter dedicated to addressing vocabulary development. Chapter 5, "Important Words Are Not Always Big and Bold: Developing Vocabulary Skills," not only shares how our teaching of vocabulary terms has changed over the years but also examines what it really means to *know* a term. Students need to not only learn content area technical terms but also know how to use the vocabulary knowledge they possess to increase their word knowledge. This chapter provides suggestions for students to develop a depth of word understanding that was not emphasized previously with rote learning of vocabulary terms. Through the use of the strategies discussed, students build their vocabulary and are able to recognize unfamiliar terms they encounter in future texts.

The last chapter in the text, Chapter 6, "Creating Writers Who Are Content Area Communicators," focuses on nurturing writing-to-learn skills. Research shows that in the past, many elementary school writing activities focused on narrative texts. Although the ELA CCSS include narrative texts, it is evident that the focus of the standards is on informational text. Within this chapter, suggestions will be provided to help students write opinion pieces, informational texts, and narrative texts. In addition, K–3 students will learn to use their knowledge of words and visuals to convey meaning.

Finally, I have included an appendix with reproducibles that might be used with the activities shared within the pages of *Powerful Content Connections*. Of course, every student and every classroom is unique. Therefore, these reproducibles should serve as a starting point. Feel free to use them as already developed, but do not hesitate to modify them as needed to meet student needs. It is my hope that the items within the appendix and the ideas shared in the chapters not only will be able to be used immediately in the classroom but also will be ones that you will want to return to again and again.

Acknowledgments

It may sound cliché, but I am indebted to the readers of this text. As I sit here writing this book, I am thankful for the teachers who read my texts and who try out the suggestions. There is nothing that makes my day better than receiving an e-mail from someone who wants to talk about the text or who has a question. Often when I write, I wonder who is out there reading the words I put on the page. I write because I love to write. I also love to hear that teachers are enjoying trying some of the ideas I share.

Of course, I am also grateful for those teachers who provided an ear and a voice to help me think through ideas. I have had some outstanding teachers walk through my classroom door as a college professor, and I am always thankful for them. I especially want to thank Chelsea Sosnowski, Christine Terrell, and Shannon Thornhill. Their ideas, enthusiasm, and willingness to help were appreciated.

CHAPTER 1

Empowering Our Earliest Literacy Learners

Have you ever heard the comment, "I can't believe what they expect students to learn at my child's grade level!"? Rather, I should rephrase that to ask, *when* did you hear the comment last? Whenever I hear it, usually at gatherings of parents on a playground or even in a grocery store line, the parents are oftentimes referring to a child in the primary grades. Because of the high expectations for our earliest learners, I have heard that more and more parents consider waiting an extra year to enroll their child in kindergarten if the child's birth date provides the option. Educational expectations are much higher than many parents experienced when they were in the primary grades because so much has changed in the world, and change continues to occur at never-before-seen speeds.

We have to maintain high expectations for early literacy learners in order to prepare them for future careers and life. Although people may argue that students in K–3 are a bit young to begin worrying about careers and life after school, we have to lay the foundation with our youngest learners so they are prepared to meet the expectations at future grade levels. As Alvermann (2001) emphasizes, everyday literacy practices are changing at unprecedented rates. For instance, we know it is not nearly enough to be able to read and comprehend printed text, but children must also be comfortable with navigating nonprint media (McPherson, 2007) such as databases, spreadsheets, blogs, and virtual field trips. These are just a few types of nonprint media young children are being introduced to in the elementary classroom. In addition, we cannot be satisfied if our children can state the main idea of a text; rather, they must be able to critically read, synthesize information, and understand the author's point of view.

At one time, most families had encyclopedias in their home. When anyone needed to know information on a topic, he or she simply looked the answer up in one of the volumes. Those times are long gone. Ikpeze and Boyd (2007) sum it up best when they refer to this overwhelming amount of information available as a "knowledge explosion" (p. 644). Students are now bombarded with information when they seek out an answer using nonprint media. They can even be bombarded by information they never planned to seek out. We want our students to be thinkers and to be able to critically analyze text they encounter through nonprint media so that they are not at the mercies of the creators of the text.

It does not seem that long ago when most of us had landline telephones, and some of us can remember when telephone answering machines became popular. Technological changes did not occur that quickly years ago. Now technology is continually changing. Our students not only have to be comfortable using the current technology, but also they must be prepared to adapt to whatever technological changes are to come. Luckily, they are "digital natives" who are growing up with technology, so the ability to use technology and apply what they know to future technological changes will not be difficult for most of them. In fact, most of our young learners are quicker to catch on to technology than we are, but being able to use technology is not enough. They must be savvy consumers of the information provided by technology. That is where we can play an important role in their use of technology.

It probably is not surprising to many of us that Avgerinou (2009) found that students spend more time engaged with technology than they spend in school. Think about the technology we see young children using: The use of iPads and smartphones is becoming much more commonplace. Therefore, we must begin incorporating technology into our lessons at the earliest grade levels and help students to be intelligent consumers of the information. They will need to understand nonprint media so that they can compete in the workplace and global market (Leu, 2000; Schmar-Dobler, 2003). There are very few jobs today that do not require technological knowledge, and jobs requiring the lowest level of technological knowledge are also often the lowest paying.

Ask your students to talk to a parent, neighbor, or other adult. Have them find out how the adults learned information when they were young. Did they use the Internet? What types of books did they use and where did they get the texts? Do they have any memories about science, social studies, or math? What type of writing did they do in school? Then have students share with the class what they learned. For very young children, you may choose to have a few adults visit the classroom and serve as a panel. Students can develop the questions ahead of time and ask the panel their questions at the time of the visit. If possible, videotape the session so the students can review what was said.

Think about what it means to be a reader, a writer, or even a literate person today. We know that the definition will not be the same today as it will be in even 10 or 20 years, and that in the future being literate will probably require even more sophisticated skills. In 2008, the National Council of Teachers of English (NCTE) changed its definition of 21st-century literacies (see www.ncte.org/positions/statements/21stcentdefinition). This definition was updated in February 2013, and I am sure the definition will continue to evolve. We must think about our vision of what it means to be literate in the 21st century and determine how our instruction can help our early literacy learners achieve that vision. One thing is definite: The younger our students are when we begin strengthening their literacy skills, the better prepared our students will be to thrive in an ever-changing world and be contributing members of society.

How the Common Core State Standards Reshape Instruction

Prior to now, most schools were guided by standards created by professional organizations targeting specific content areas. As teachers, we often focused on the standards developed by the National Council of Teachers of Mathematics, the National Council for the Social Studies (NCSS), and the National Science Teachers Association (NSTA). However, that is changing for those involved in the educational field, and the Common Core State Standards (CCSS) are now influencing our classroom instruction.

The CCSS are rigorous for all students from kindergarten through high school because the standards are designed to prepare students for college and careers. Across the grade-level expectations of the English Language Arts (ELA) standards, the CCSS emphasize the importance of understanding complex texts, reading informational texts, writing to learn, building vocabulary skills, and creating powerful literacy connections throughout the content areas. These areas of emphasis will be the focus of this book. Because connections between literacy and the content areas may not occur automatically, especially in primary grades, the ideas in this text enable K–3 students to make those connections while meeting the ELA CCSS.

In order for students to develop disciplinary literacy, or literacy skills specific to the individual content areas, we must reexamine and reframe our literacy instruction for the earliest literacy learners. Preparing students for college and career readiness and the ability to be successful outside the classroom requires specialized skills. In other words, students must read, write, and think like scientists, historians, and other specialists—and it is our job to provide the instructional support and content knowledge to get them on their way.

Synthesizing Foundational Skills With Other Aspects of Literacy Development

For our K–3 students, we must pave the way for disciplinary literacy skill development through appropriate experiences and materials. To begin, our children need strong foundational skills. We must explicitly teach print concepts, phonological awareness, phonics, word recognition, and fluency so that children can build and strengthen their basic literacy skills. The CCSS recognize the importance of these skills, and an entire section of the ELA standards is dedicated to the discussion of foundational skills. These skills are vital for our students to be able to comprehend more sophisticated texts they will encounter throughout the content areas.

However, we do not need to develop foundation skills prior to emphasizing content area literacy connections, and there is no reason to focus solely on foundational skills prior to incorporating other types of literacy activity into our K–3 classrooms. As we are developing these foundational skills, we can introduce materials such as digital and informational texts into our classroom, enhance our students' development of technical vocabulary, and encourage writing to learn.

Furthermore, literacy skills are not meant to be taught in a sequential and isolated manner. Because reading, writing, listening, and viewing are skills we use interchangeably as literate adults, we should not attempt to separate them for our youngest learners. By keeping our eye on the bigger picture—the goal of developing literate adults and remembering how we use literacy in our day-to-day lives—we can help our students develop the full range of literacy skills they need to succeed in the world. While our instruction in primary grades should focus explicitly on foundational skills, it should be done in an environment where the simultaneous growth of other aspects of literacy are encouraged and valued.

Increasing Emphasis on Informational Text

Even our youngest learners, who enjoy shared reading experiences, can gain a great deal of knowledge through listening to and discussing informational text. Informational text is the type of text that adults engage with most often on a regular basis and is the type of material that children will be exposed to the most. It has important characteristics that make it unique. Duke and Bennett-Armistead (2003) explain that such text not only provides information about the world, but also has "particular linguistic features such as headings and technical vocabulary to help accomplish that purpose" (p. 16).

By introducing the youngest of students to tables, headings, tables of contents, and diagrams, we are demystifying many of the features they encounter in informational texts. Often students at higher grade levels struggle with content area material because they have limited experience with such texts. We can help our students be successful with informational texts by engaging them with such texts at a young age. For example, not only can our K–3 students enjoy listening to us share the texts, but also they can create whole-class informational texts using information gained through digital texts. Through this process, we can also introduce our students to complex texts.

Many teachers I know are concerned that this means their early learners will not have an opportunity to become familiar with the world of fairy tales and stories that were an important part of their childhood. Let us be clear on this point: Exposing students to more informational texts does not mean that we no longer share our love of poetry, narrative, and drama with our K–3 students, but it does mean incorporating a wider variety of texts into our classrooms.

Building Technical Vocabulary Skills

Although learning to recognize high-frequency words by sight is an important focus in the early years, K–3 students can also begin to think about content area terms and technical vocabulary. As they familiarize themselves with technical terms through listening activities, these words will become part of their oral vocabulary. Strengthening children's vocabulary knowledge and assisting them with using this newfound knowledge to recognize other content area terms they encounter is important.

Often when we hear the term *technical vocabulary*, we envision long, polysyllabic words encountered in high school content area textbooks. However, that is not the case. Even our youngest learners are confronted with technical vocabulary. Technical vocabulary consists of words they do not use on a daily basis in their oral language and terms they probably encounter for the first time when they talk and learn about a specific content area subject. For young learners we can introduce, teach, and reinforce the technical terms they encounter in specific content areas. As students are exploring topics such as weather or plants in science or community workers and continents in social studies, you can draw their attention to technical words and participate in activities to develop and strengthen their content area vocabulary.

Encouraging Writing to Learn

We also see a growing emphasis on writing to learn in the CCSS. As adults, we often write to inform or persuade others. We draft e-mails, reports, and directions. We write the steps colleagues, friends, and family members must follow in order to participate in certain activities. Likewise, many careers require that employees be able to write summaries, how-to explanations, persuasive documents, and other types of informational text. How many adults do we know who write stories regularly? Although an extremely small number of our children may grow up to write romance novels or children's stories, the vast majority will not. However, all children will need to be able to write informational texts—simply participating in day-to-day living activities requires reading and writing informational text. Therefore, while students at all grade levels are expected to be able to write narratives, the writing emphasis must shift from writing stories to writing to learn.

As we may know, writing activities do not occur after reading skills have developed, and through writing experiences, our youngest children can begin building their reading and spelling skills. Writing to learn can begin while children are learning to write. Often early learners begin learning about writing by dictating thoughts that adults transcribe or by drawing pictures or an initial sound they hear in words. Through these shared experiences, students can focus on content area topics they are studying and begin to understand that writing can serve a variety of purposes. Students can also create local text that ties to the content areas (See Chapter 2 for more information on local text). Local text helps K–3 learners to understand the importance of writing to communicate and serves as a valuable purpose for their writing.

Content Area Instruction With Young Literacy Learners

In the not-too-distant past, many people equated content area instruction with older students. In fact, most universities have a content area reading course, but the course is designed for those wishing to teach middle school and high school students. Often those desiring to be elementary teachers were taught strategies that were designed to be used across the content areas, with little thought being given to the demands of the specific disciplines. However, that thinking began changing because of research. Shanahan and Shanahan (2008) drew a great deal of attention to content area instruction when they developed a three-tiered model of literacy skills.

At the lowest level of the pyramid are basic literacy skills. Many of us recognize these as foundational literacy skills. These basic skills are traditionally taught during the primary grades. At this level, students learn to understand concepts of print, begin to develop automaticity with basic sight words, and familiarize themselves with the key components of a story. In addition, students learn the basic elements of story grammar and are introduced to the elements of a plot. These are very basic skills and, until now, basic literacy skills were often the focus of our early literacy instruction.

The next level in Shanahan and Shanahan's diagram is referred to as intermediate literacy. At this level, students learn to read polysyllabic words, expand their sight vocabulary, develop metacognitive awareness, increase their vocabulary, and read a wider range of texts. According to Shanahan and Shanahan (2008), most students are able to attain this level by the end of middle school. However, as we can see, the skills at the intermediate literacy level are not linked to specific content areas.

The top level of the pyramid is where we see disciplinary literacy skills. These skills are more sophisticated but much less generalizable than those found at the lower levels on the pyramid. Students are expected to be able to read and view content area text in the same manner that scientists, historians, and mathematicians view it. Unlike content area instruction, disciplinary literacy skills require teachers to think about the skills needed to work with specific content area text.

Although Shanahan and Shanahan (2008) note that disciplinary literacy skills are seldom taught at the middle school and high school levels but must be addressed at those levels, the CCSS and the demands of today's global marketplace force us to emphasize disciplinary literacy much earlier in a child's education. As we develop our students' oral, visual, and written skills, let us think about how our literacy instruction is preparing our young students to develop disciplinary literacy skills.

Let us look at some of the key points we must consider as we empower our early literacy learners. As we read and reflect on each of these points, we can think about how the ideas fit into our current classroom instruction and how we might make modifications to create even more powerful literacy connections across all content areas. These points will be reinforced throughout the pages of this text.

Incorporate Visuals and Technology

As teachers, we cannot ignore the potential of visuals in the classroom. As we are well aware, our students today are bombarded with images (Conley, 2008). As our early literacy learners get older, they will be immersed in even more media. There is no way to stop that, and I do not think anyone wants to discourage students from engaging in quality media. However, the keyword in that sentence is *quality*. We are all aware that much of the digital text our students may encounter may not be the highest quality. Therefore, it is our job as their teachers to help our K–3 students learn to be savvy consumers of such text. Considine, Horton, and Moorman (2009) have shown that students must be able to comprehend and be aware of the creators' intent, and this is true with even our youngest students. The ELA CCSS recognize the important role that technology plays in our children's lives today, and technology is woven throughout the CCSS.

It does not seem that long ago when one of parents' biggest concerns was monitoring the content of commercials and television programming their children viewed. Although it seemed like a huge task at the time, it was not that difficult because children had access to televisions in limited settings. Whether little Suzy, our child's best friend, had parents who let her watch certain television channels was considered a major issue. However, television, and the material it showed, was limited mostly to the home environment. Now we have a much larger amount of nonprint media students are exposed to at the earliest of ages. Almost anywhere children go they have access to digital texts—and all the advertising and consumer-focused messaging that come with it.

Nowadays we have much more to be concerned about than the visual information children view during television shows. Students now view videos or access websites on the Internet almost anywhere on tablets and smartphones. They access digital texts at schools, in the library, and while passing time waiting for siblings to participate in classes, for parents to get cars fixed, and even for their restaurant meals to arrive. Our K–3 learners do not even have to "get" to a specific place to view nonprint media. Many are connected while traveling from one place to another on a plane, train, car, or even on foot.

Therefore, we must focus on the visuals and technology available. If we do not plan meaningful activities and experiences to incorporate visuals into our classroom so that our young children develop visual literacy skills, we are neglecting an important aspect of literacy development. The power of technology does not reside in the materials themselves available in the classroom, but rather in how we, as teachers, use such materials to help students learn. We cannot wait any longer to incorporate visual literacy into the classroom. As Flynt and Brozo (2010) state, "The digitally connected world is here and now" (p. 526).

Encourage Questioning

Because our young children live in an information age and will be continually inundated with messages telling them how they should think, act, and feel, they must learn to interpret and think about messages and decide what to do with the information they encounter. Such text is not limited to digital texts. Authors of printed text also seek to have readers behave in a specific way. We must encourage our students to ask questions and think about the content in texts. Whether we are sharing a text orally with a kindergarten class or asking slightly older children to read parts of an informational text, we must ask the children to critically evaluate what they read. They can tie information they read to what they already know about the topic or examine what other sources say about the topic. Students must learn to constantly ask themselves, Does it make sense? Is it possible? Why is the author writing this text? How does this information tie to other things I know? According to many in the field (e.g., Soares & Wood, 2010; VanSledright, 2002; Wineburg & Martin, 2004), social studies can be a great place to help students develop questioning skills and become critical consumers of information.

Many of us grew up believing that if something was in print then it must be true. That has not changed much for students over the years. In fact, research shows that older adolescents read history texts and assume that the information they are reading is factual (Hynd-Shanahan, Holschuh, & Hubbard, 2005). However, as adults we know now that is not true. You cannot take what you read at face value. Instead you must look at both the source and the purpose of the text and consider what other sources say on the topic.

Often teachers struggle to teach students at older grade levels to question what they read in texts and to compare multiple sources. It is not only true with social studies texts. Research conducted by Rice (2002) shows that students often accept information presented in science texts as accurate even if it is not. It is tough to change students' ways of thinking after they spent years in school believing what they read was true; the belief is embedded so deeply into their way of thinking that they consider the author of the text the authority on a topic. Also, in content area materials text can reveal author bias and can be written to persuade listeners or readers to respond in a certain way. So the questioning process really must begin at the earliest grade levels, when students are more apt to ask questions. We must work hard to empower our youngest learners to realize that information in texts is not always factual and true (VanSledright, 2002), and we need to teach them how to compare sources to find factual answers and identify bias.

Rethink Materials

Many of us equate early childhood with the wonderful world of fables and folk tales. We have fond memories of the vivid images conjured up in our mind as the teacher wove magical elements throughout the amazing tales. Those moments when we became aesthetically involved with a story, or part of the story experience, are powerful. These are still important experiences to help children develop a love of reading and enthusiasm for writing. However, students must learn to read narrative stories and informational texts in very different ways.

Rosenblatt (1938), a leading theorist in literacy, explains how we read with either an aesthetic stance, in order to become part of the story experience, or with an efferent stance, to take away information. We can help our young literacy learners to understand the stances, so that they set a purpose when reading a text. It is imperative that students realize that they read different types of materials differently.

For instance, think about how students read a science experiment, which is a typical informational text found in a K–3 classroom, versus a fable, another common text. As students read a science experiment, they must understand the sequential structure used in the text, pay attention to details in the steps, and think about how their prior knowledge of science ties to what they are doing and learning. However, if students are reading a fable, they will probably be working with a genre that is more familiar to them. They can immerse themselves in the fantasy elements of the story because they will not have to pay attention to technical vocabulary, and they will not need to be as concerned with their prior knowledge on a topic. Our students cannot approach both fictional and informational texts with the same stance or they will not be getting the most from either experience.

Greenwood (2004) writes about how older students hit the wall when they are expected to engage with content area texts. We can eliminate that issue by rethinking the types of text we use in the K–3 classroom and by helping students to realize that not all texts are viewed the same way.

By engaging our youngest learners with informational text, we can help them to be successful beyond the walls of the classroom.

Restructure Read-Alouds

The merits of using class time to read aloud to students have been discussed for years, and read-alouds continue to play a significant role in many early childhood classrooms. For many years, reading aloud was encouraged because during that time the students were exposed to fluent reading and quality literature. Many of us are familiar with Jim Trelease, a man who became a common name among parents and educators when he created *The Read-Aloud Handbook* (Trelease, 2013), a very successful text now in its seventh edition. We know there are many benefits to reading aloud, and with such a limited amount of time with our students, we need to maximize teachable moments. The time during our day when we read aloud can serve as an excellent time to incorporate informational text into the classroom with even the earliest learners.

For K–3 learners, the read-aloud experience can serve as an opportunity to build not only prior content knowledge, but also technical vocabulary (Webster, 2009). During the read-aloud experience, we can expose our students to text structures commonly seen in the content areas such as cause and effect, descriptive, and chronological. As students examine texts, we can draw their attention to linguistic features commonly seen in informational text such as headings, fonts, and visuals (Jalongo, 2006), and we can remind them to question the material that is being read. All of these activities will help students to meet the CCSS and allow us to make the most of the time we spend reading aloud with our students.

Blur the Dividing Lines

Let us think about the types of tasks and texts we engage with on a daily basis. When we shop, create a household budget, assemble purchases, and read charts or tables, we are weaving together our literacy skills and content area knowledge. If we do not separate literacy from the content areas as adults, why do we expect our children to do so? Children do not see divisions among the areas, but as adults we create these artificial divisions with space, time, and materials (Altieri, 2010). Students often learn in school that now they will have reading time, and this time will be followed by x, y, and z. If time allows during a very busy and full day, there might be social studies later on.

In order to help our students to begin thinking like mathematicians, scientists, and historians, we must blur the dividing lines. By doing so, we will also be addressing the issue of too many subjects in too little time. Time is always a precious commodity in classrooms, and when we choose to break everything up into the smallest possible unit, it becomes impossible to address everything that must be taught in school. Instead of segmenting the day, we must teach reading, writing, and thinking skills across the content areas in which our students engage. There is only one way to do that. We can no longer teach discrete subjects; rather, we must embed literacy skills within the content areas. Adults are the ones who create the dividing lines between literacy and other content areas, so we need to be the ones who remove them.

Research strongly supports blurring the lines between literacy and the content areas. Some in the educational field believe that students who learn to comprehend text while learning content area material develop stronger literacy skills and more content knowledge (e.g., Reutzel, Smith, & Fawson, 2005; Williams, Stafford, Lauer, Hall, & Pollini, 2009). This is true at the youngest of ages. According to research conducted by Connor et al. (2010), second graders with weak literacy and science skills have been shown to improve as much in scientific knowledge as those students with stronger skills. Also, young children have been shown to grasp mathematical concepts much more quickly with mathematical text read-alouds accompanying other mathematical activities (Casey, Kersh, & Young, 2004). Of course, the benefits for students are not solely academic. Third graders who were taught reading and science in an integrated manner were found not only to be more self-motivated to read, but also to have a much better self-efficacy for reading (Wigfield, Guthrie, Tonks, & Perencevich, 2004). As we motivate and develop our students' confidence with a variety of texts, we will be providing them with reading values that will last a lifetime.

As everyone knows, we learn by doing. You cannot learn to swim without getting into the water. The ability to become readers, writers, and thinkers of scientific material, historical essays, and other content is possible only if students have the opportunity to develop literacy skills through the content areas. Students must also realize that within each content area, text can vary. For example, our earliest learners must realize that scientific writing varies. They can examine how a simple science experiment is written and compare it with a brief text encouraging them to recycle. Further, students can examine timelines and other visuals found in social studies text, view primary sources, and compare and contrast brief texts read aloud on the same topic. It is only through these types of practices that our students will experience literacy growth in each content area.

Raise Expectations

We must raise our student expectations. The ELA CCSS are intense. They are demanding. Educators have expressed concern about whether it is realistic for children to attain the standards. However, the CCSS cannot be ignored. Although there are many arguments about the CCSS and whether states should have adopted them, the reality is that we can better use the time spent arguing a viewpoint or complaining about the decision by finding the best possible way to successfully implement the standards in the classroom.

Often in the past when classroom texts seemed too difficult for students to read, they would be taught through other means. The teacher might explain the material in an easier-to-understand format or allow students to demonstrate their understanding through other modalities. I remember when I taught the primary grades and was adamant that the classroom text for social studies was too difficult for my students. I was encouraged by many well-meaning educators to put the texts away and teach the content through other means.

Although there is nothing inherently wrong with modifying our teaching to meet individual student needs, the CCSS require that students not only independently access the information in challenging text beginning in second grade, but also that they be able to communicate the information they gain from the text. Therefore, we will have to teach students effective strategies so that they can unlock the information found in the texts. Even more, we have to help students understand effective strategies well enough so that they can independently use the strategies as they progress through more difficult texts. This is not easy. We must provide scaffolding, monitor our students, and know how to effectively give them more and more responsibility for their learning. As will be discussed in Chapter 4, through a gradual release of responsibility model, students can build their understanding of texts on their own.

Because we are raising our own expectations, we will also have to raise students' expectations for themselves. Students must believe in their abilities and have the confidence that they can work with content area texts. As discussed previously, with the ELA CCSS there is no way to avoid challenging text. These texts may seem overwhelming to students, but as they continue through the grade levels, the textual demands will become greater. We can begin to expose students to more challenging text and provide them with strategies for working with the text in our K–3 classrooms.

Differentiate Instruction

This is a necessary component of any effective classroom instruction. Although differentiating instruction has always been important because of the diversity of students in our classrooms (e.g., struggling readers, gifted and talented students, English learners), the high expectations of the CCSS reinforce the importance of differentiating the amount and type of support provided to each of our students. As with any classroom, some students may already possess a specific skill or have the knowledge necessary to successfully meet a standard, while other students may need additional time or a modification in instruction in order to achieve success. Although it is difficult to balance the needs of our students with the content we wish to teach, it is imperative that we do so in order to create effective literacy learners.

The CCSS explicitly state the standards the students at each grade level are expected to meet or what the students must learn. They do not tell us how to teach the material or get the students to the end result. We all know from our life experiences that there are multiple paths to getting from Point A to Point B. Taking into consideration the individual child is a must. Through continuous informal assessment and documentation of our students' literacy skills and modification of instruction based on what is working and not working with them, we can differentiate instruction so that children can successfully meet the standards. By providing appropriate scaffolding, we develop our students' confidence and continue to challenge them at the same time.

We teachers are the key players. The CCSS are provided, but we must develop the road map to help all students get from their current location to the desired destination. We have that power. We are the only ones capable of making the CCSS a reality in the classroom. We must continually ask ourselves, What should I do when I get to the classroom tomorrow to help nurture readers, writers, and thinkers who can be successful in later grades, their careers, and life?

The Role of Powerful Connections in the Classroom Context

In order to make the ELA CCSS a reality in our K–3 classrooms, we must examine the type of connections we are making between the content areas and literacy skills. In Table 1, we see four levels of connections. Although the levels are hierarchical, it is not necessary to progress step by step through the levels in order to create powerful connections.

Table 1. Levels of Content Area Connections

Level	Title	Description
1	Superficial	• Some content area texts available • Connections are made by chance • Content literacy and literacy seen as discrete skills
2	Developing	• Adequate high-quality content area texts available • Little differentiation made between types of text • Explicit connections are few and far between
3	Advanced	• Adequate high-quality content area texts available • Differentiation of narrative and informative texts • Informative texts are used as often as any other type of text in the classroom • Literacy skills are often woven through content areas
4	Powerful	• Adequate high-quality content area texts available • Differentiation of narrative and informative texts and specific content area texts • Informative texts are often used in the classroom • Purposeful planning engages students with disciplinary literacy skills

The table is designed to get teachers thinking about and discussing current classroom levels of content connections. By reflecting on the key points discussed in the table and critically examining our K–3 classrooms, we might have a better idea of what changes should occur in the classroom environment in order to progress to the Powerful Level of connections, or Level 4.

At the lowest level, Level 1 or the Superficial Level, appropriate content area materials may be available, but explicit connections are not made between topics taught in the content areas and literacy activities or materials available in the classroom. While some informational books might be found in the classroom, there are many more faction (see Chapter 2 for more detail) and fictional texts available with which students might engage. When the read-aloud experience occurs, rarely is an informational text chosen to share. Students might point out that a topic they have been studying in class ties to the material in a text, or they may mention commonalities they notice between two social studies or science texts. However, a key component of a classroom with powerful connections, the planning necessary to allow the students to develop disciplinary literacy skills, is missing.

Beginning at Level 2, or the Developing Level, on through Level 4, the Powerful Level, the classroom has adequate high-quality content area texts available on a variety of topics. By looking at these three levels, we can see clearly that the availability of extensive materials does not necessarily influence the level of connections. Without proper planning by the teacher, connections can continue to function at Level 2 indefinitely despite the quality materials available.

At the Developing Level, one might find a number of informational texts in the classroom library about science and social studies topics students are engaging with in the classroom. Also, when selecting a text to read aloud or share with students, the teacher on occasion selects an informational text. However, the class refers to all of the texts used in the classroom as *stories*. Little differentiation is made between narrative texts and informational texts. Students, who are beginning to write, sometimes write about a topic currently studied in the content area, but that is the extent of the connection between the content areas and literacy skills. Although the materials and experiences are available, the connections are still few and far between. Literacy instruction and the content areas are rarely woven together. Instead, the content areas and literacy skills seem to be running on parallel paths throughout the instruction.

At Level 3 or the Advanced Level, we see some common components that make this level stand out from the Developing Level. First, an effort is made by the teacher to point out the differences between narrative and informational texts. Even though the students are young, they are learning that narrative stories have characters and a plot, while informational books have certain linguistic features, people or animals, and a text structure. Often the teacher chooses an informational text that ties to a content area to read aloud. Whether students are engaging in sustained silent reading, shared reading, or any other type of textual experience, they are just as apt to be reading informational texts as narrative texts. Often students are developing writing skills through writing-to-learn activities about content material. The students may be writing the steps to a science experiment they just completed (as a whole class or in groups depending on the grade level) or creating a biography about the firefighter who visited their classroom.

At the highest level, Level 4 or the Powerful Level, we see powerful connections. Students are not only learning to differentiate between narrative and informational texts, but also they are realizing that there are differences even within specific content areas. Students are learning, for instance, that science texts often contain important visuals and diagrams, and that because of these visuals they often have to read science texts differently from other texts. Although reading left to right and top to bottom is important, students realize that they have to be able to look at words and visuals and draw meaning through information provided by both within a text. They also realize that content areas have different demands: Reading in social studies is not the same as reading in science. For example, often in social studies students have to think even more about the author's purpose in writing the text, and students are developing an understanding of primary documents and the importance of the information they provide for readers.

A powerful connection tries to make the most of teachable moments in the classroom and opportunities to help students understand that text varies. The text of choice to read aloud is often an informational text. It is not unusual for the teacher to take advantage of the time used to read aloud texts to model a think-aloud, showing how good readers might approach the text. The teacher not only draws attention to the important linguistic features, but also demonstrates how those features can be used to help readers develop a better understanding of the book. During individual writing time (or perhaps during the writing of a class-dictated text with very young children), students talk about how photos, a table of contents, and other key features might be used in their own writing that ties to the content area topics being studied. When presented with a literacy task, the students think about the audience and why they are writing or reading text. These connections take place because of prior modeling and planning by the teacher. The teacher makes informed decisions and purposefully plans materials and experiences that will engage the students and build disciplinary literacy skills.

TRY IT OUT

Review Table 1 with other teachers. Discuss the level at which you believe your classroom is currently functioning. Then set a higher level as a realistic goal for your classroom this year. Think about what is keeping your room from moving to more powerful content area connections. Fold a sheet of paper in two lengthwise and then unfold it. In the left column, write down two or three changes that are necessary in classroom instruction so that the goal is attainable. In the right column, list a few realistic, specific ideas for how you can make each of those changes a reality. Refer to the created list at the beginning of each month or thematic unit so that you do not stray from your vision. If you struggle to move to a higher level, rethink your practical ideas for doing so, and try to determine what is obstructing the change.

REFLECTING BACK AS WE MOVE FORWARD

In order to prepare our K–3 students to meet the ELA CCSS and the literacy demands they will encounter as adults, we must have purposeful teaching. Purposeful teaching is teaching that targets the literacy skills our students must develop and provides opportunities for them to make powerful content area connections. It does not necessarily require additional time or money to make our classrooms with superficial connections become ones with powerful connections. It takes planning with a purpose. We must purposefully create connections focusing on disciplinary literacy skills and engaging readers. Powerful connections do not happen by chance. They are planned.

The remaining chapters in this book provide important ideas for making these powerful content area connections a reality. As we close our classroom door at the end of each day, we want to know that we did everything possible that day to nurture readers, writers, and thinkers who can be successful in later grades, their careers, and life. Powerful connections make that possibility a reality.

CHAPTER 2

The Increasing Emphasis on Materials: Teaching With High-Quality Informational Texts

Although we know that teachers and students play key roles in the classroom, there is an increasing emphasis placed on material usage in instruction. This may be because there are more materials available today that can be incorporated into our lessons. We no longer are limited to printed texts, so the task of locating, evaluating, and using diverse texts can be a time-consuming process. Research is showing that often the type of texts used with young children in the classroom and the types of text that they will encounter later in life and outside of school are very different. The importance of using texts that children see outside of the classroom context and texts that will prepare them for future literacy experiences is vital.

According to Venezky (2000), informational text is the most prevalent type of text we encounter as adults. Therefore, as teachers, we can use this type of text that children see in the home environment to make powerful connections to text in the school environment. Even if some of our students are not using or seeing a great deal of informational text at home, connections can still be made between the topics discussed in narrative texts and students' own interests with informational printed texts and digital texts. This is an excellent time to reinforce to students why informational text is used and to make the connection between the types of reading adults do and the type of reading they do. Further, researchers who have worked with students from low socioeconomic status (SES) backgrounds have stressed the benefits that can be gained by bridging the gap of home and school literacy environments (Duke & Purcell-Gates, 2003).

Whether we flip through the pages of an educational journal or search for literacy articles online, we are bound to encounter the term *multiple literacies*. This term refers in part to "the many and varied ways that people read and write in their lives" (Purcell-Gates, 2002, p. 376). Multiple literacies can include printed texts such as the writing on a cereal box, grocery store fliers, or even road signs. It can also include nonprint media such as movies, plays, and paintings.

Although drama, art, and music should be used to connect and enrich our students' experiences in the classroom and beyond and to encourage our students to explore areas of interest more in depth, the focus of this text is on the use of informational text. As we work with and engage our K–3 learners with content material, we must think about printed texts and digital sources. Through the careful use of such text, we can create powerful content area connections and target key aspects of the ELA CCSS.

Focusing Our Students' Attention on Text

Young children need to realize why printed text is important and how it relates to the world outside the classroom walls. We must help them to understand why we read different types of printed text and draw their attention to informational text, in particular. According to Moss (2005), the increased attention in the educational field to standards-based instruction, standardized testing, and technology results in an increased emphasis on informational text and a shift in the use of such texts to the elementary grades. If we are using informational texts more frequently as part of our classroom instruction, then we want students to see that these texts play an important role in their lives.

Let's begin by looking at what we can learn about our own experiences with printed text. Make a chart similar to the one shown in Figure 1. Share the chart with your students and, as a class, brainstorm additional types of printed text people encounter. Discuss each type of text and where students might encounter it, why it might be used, and its importance in their lives.

Give students the Text Is All Around Me Chart found on page 160 in the Appendix to take home. If they encounter a specific type of text, they can note it in the appropriate column. Our older students might want to write a detail about the type of text found or where they encountered the text. For example, third-grade students might choose to write the name of the stories or texts they read or the purpose of the instructions they saw. Allow enough time for students to engage with diverse texts. Two to four

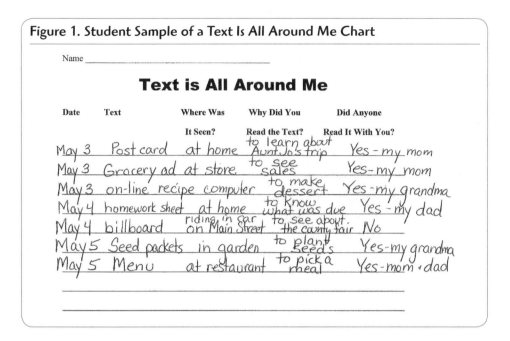

Figure 1. Student Sample of a Text Is All Around Me Chart

Name _____

Text is All Around Me

Date	Text	Where Was It Seen?	Why Did You Read the Text?	Did Anyone Read It With You?
May 3	Post card	at home	to learn about Aunt Jo's trip	Yes – my mom
May 3	Grocery ad	at store	to see sales	Yes – my mom
May 3	on-line recipe	computer	to make dessert	Yes – my grandma
May 4	homework sheet	at home	to know what was due	Yes – my dad
May 4	billboard	riding in car on Main Street	to see about the county fair	No
May 5	Seed packets	in garden	to plant seeds	Yes – my grandma
May 5	Menu	at restaurant	to pick a meal	Yes – mom & dad

days should be enough time for them to complete the charts. Consider sending home the chart over a weekend.

Also consider sending home a note to the parents or guardians of the youngest learners to let them know that the class is looking at the types of printed text encountered. Encourage them to sit with their child once or twice each day to see what types of text he or she has encountered. If the children and parents wait until the day the chart is due to complete it, they will have forgotten many experiences that they had with text. A sample letter to parents and guardians is included on page 161 of the Appendix. Don't forget to make a Text Is All Around Me Chart for yourself!

Ask the class to return the Text Is All Around Me Chart on the assigned date. As the teacher, be sure to bring your own completed copy back to class to share and discuss with your students. You are not only playing an active role in the lesson, but also modeling that you value text and the important role it plays in your life. (Not to mention that it will also dispel the belief young children have that teachers live in the school.) Lead a class discussion about the results.

Ask the students to talk about the types of text they encountered. Where did they see the printed words? Was it a story read before bedtime or while waiting in the doctor's office? What did students see in the newspaper or online? What was the reason for reading the text—to entertain or read for fun or to learn something? Was anyone else involved while they looked at the text?

Students can talk about the purposes texts serve, and they also may talk about the fact that sometimes text is read with others. This can be an opportunity to talk about the importance of looking at text with others and the social nature of reading. Be sure to record how many types of text children encountered on the class chart. You could connect this activity with mathematics by helping students create a chart to see which types of printed materials were viewed the most and the least. Many young children encounter a good amount of informational text in the home. In fact, research conducted with young children by Caswell and Duke (1998) found that nonnarrative texts were more consistent with boys' home literacies than were narrative texts.

As an extension for this activity, students might ask an adult to complete the Text Is All Around Me Chart. You might ask the adults to note if the text was printed or digital (read on a smartphone, tablet, or computer), reinforcing the important role digital text plays in many adults' lives. Compare the information on the children's and the adults' charts. Talk about the similarities and differences between the types of texts encountered by adults and by children.

Most likely, there will be a lot of informational text read by adults. There may also be a fair amount of informational text read by children—on signs, in newspapers, or in books. Take this opportunity to focus students' attention on why we read informational text and how it is a necessary part of our daily lives. Adults might read the text so they can organize and plan events, understand a politician's view on a topic, or fix a lawn mower. Children need to read or have someone help them read informational text so that they can follow directions to build a model car or understand the television guide to know which programs are being broadcast. The purpose of the Text Is All Around Me activity is to get students to think about the texts they encounter on a regular basis and to realize how often the texts they engage with in the world convey information.

In the primary grades, our young students can't wait to grow up and participate in grown-up activities. How many times do we hear our own children, nieces, or nephews beg to help us with projects or activities that are designed for those who are older? I can remember many of the young students I worked with over the years enjoying *Jamal's Busy Day* (Hudson, 1991) because the plot parallels young Jamal's day and his parents' day; both Jamal and his parents attend meetings, complete projects, and work hard. Jamal shows that they both have very busy days. By helping our students to understand how important informational text is in the world around them, it makes that type of text that much more enticing to them. Informational text will also build content knowledge while enhancing students' literacy skills in the primary grades—a win-win!

A Shifting Focus to Informational Text

The ELA CCSS are focusing on informational text for a reason. Duke (2000) conducted a groundbreaking study that set the educational community abuzz with the urgency of incorporating informational text into the classroom. In her study, she examined 20 first-grade classrooms in the Boston area representing both low- and high-SES classrooms. The results were alarming and continue to be a source of discussion in the educational community. Duke found that first graders were exposed to only 3.6 minutes of informational text each day during their "whole class written language activities" (p. 215). Many of us still toss that figure around in our mind. How can that be possible? Students spend more time walking in line to and from other special areas and probably even waiting to use the restroom.

What concerns me even more is that while many of us know about the study and the limited amount of time the first graders spent with informational text, the limited amount of time with informational text wasn't consistent for all students. Even more alarming is that Duke (2000) found the text usage varied according to the student's socioeconomic status. Students from "traditionally disenfranchised social groups" (p. 202) had even less interaction with informational texts. Often those children are already struggling to meet educational expectations when they enter school, and yet once in school they are then experiencing less exposure than other students to the type of text that will help them to be successful for future careers and life.

The results of Duke's study are, unfortunately, not unique. Other studies reveal similar grim findings. For example, Kamberelis (1999) found that students in kindergarten, first grade, and second grade are more familiar with narrative texts than other genres. This is also true with our earliest learners. Yopp and Yopp (2006) examined 167 texts that were read aloud by preschool teachers and found that only 5% were informational texts. When researchers recently took a closer look at the types of texts early childhood teachers are using in read-alouds, they reviewed a much larger group who taught in two states. However, their research results confirmed that narrative was in fact the most often read genre and that informational read-alouds composed only 17% of the time teachers spent reading aloud (Pentimonti, Zucker, Justice, & Kaderavek, 2010). We all know this is not enough time, but I hope the results of these studies will serve as motivation to ensure that informational text plays a greater role in our classrooms. We must provide a wider variety of texts for our young students. With statistics like these, our early learners will never have enough access to informational texts to become familiar and comfortable enough with them to navigate successfully or meet the ELA CCSS.

The Issue of Engagement

We all want our children to develop a love for reading and literacy, and engaging them with texts is how we do that. Regardless of whether our K–3 students are reading aesthetically or efferently (see Chapter 1 for a discussion of aesthetic and efferent), we want them to be interested in the texts they encounter. Years ago, people thought that fictional components were necessary in text so that young children would be engaged with content matter (Giblin, 2000). However, we now know that does not appear to be true. Educators and researchers have confirmed that young children will engage with quality informational texts that are connected to their learning or interests (e.g., Caswell & Duke, 1998; Pappas, 1993).

Articles and books have been written about getting boys hooked on reading and keeping them interested in reading. Informational texts may help with that process. Brassell (2006) has shown that nonfiction texts are especially appealing to boys. Chapman, Filipenko, McTavish, and Shapiro (2007) have also shown that boys prefer informational text. In fact, research shows that children, including those hard-to-reach reluctant readers, prefer informational text and will choose to read such texts even when other types are introduced (Collard, 2003). This research should put to rest the concern about whether our K–3 children can and will engage with informational texts.

A Caution About Faction

Often we think that if a book conveys information, it is informational. However, recent research (Pentimonti et al., 2010) with preschoolers reveals that when teachers do read informative text, it is more often a mix of narrative and informational than strictly informational. Many of the primary teachers I work with believe they are using informational text, but when I ask them what informational texts they are using, I find it is actually a great deal of *faction*.

Faction is not the same as informational text. Faction is a blend of facts and fiction (Avery, 2003). Faction is not new—many of us remember reading such texts when we were in elementary school. Often the goal of these texts is to convey information, but there is also a lot of fiction in the narrative. For example, students learn about dental hygiene from a crocodile's view, or they may learn about how plants grow through the observant eye of insects that watch it all take place. The problem is that children can have difficulty discerning what is factual and what is fictional. Therefore, many people caution against using such texts (Bamford, Kristo, & Lyon, 2002; Smith, 2001).

I am not saying faction texts should be barred from the classroom—we all use them at one time or another. However, we all need to be aware of the difference between informational texts and faction, and we need to ensure that faction makes up only a small percentage of the books we use. If we share faction with students, the least we can do is make sure that they understand which aspects of the text are fictionalized and which are factual (Gill, 2009). The important thing to remember is that informational texts do not include fictional elements.

The Difference Between Nonfiction and Informational Text

Many times we use the terms *nonfiction* and *informational text* interchangeably. They are not the same. Both nonfiction and informational text attempt to convey information about the world from someone with expertise on the subject to someone wanting to learn about the topic. However, informational texts are actually a type of nonfiction text. Duke (2000) provides us with an easy way to differentiate between nonfiction and informational texts. Informational texts not only provide us with information, but also have certain linguistic features and technical vocabulary. These linguistic features might be photo captions, figures, graphs, tables, tables of contents, glossaries, unique fonts to emphasize words, and headings. In addition to these linguistic features, Duke (2000) notes that informational texts often have generic nouns, technical vocabulary, and a specific text structure (cause and effect, chronological, etc.). The purpose of this chapter is to ensure a solid understanding of the types of text discussed in this book, but in Chapter 4, we will discuss in detail suggestions for teaching these features of complex informational text.

A Closer Look at Linguistic Features

Let's look at linguistic features. These features are one aspect of text that differentiates an informational text from other types of text. The features can vary widely according to the reading level of the text, the topic, and the content area. The following are some of the linguistic features readers may encounter in informational text:

• indexes	• labeled diagrams	• page numbers
• maps and keys	• tables of contents	• appendixes
• captions	• headings and subheadings	• timelines
• tables	• graphs	• flowcharts
• electronic menus	• icons	• glossaries
• fonts/bold print	• sidebars and hyperlinks	

One thing is obvious from this list: There are a lot of linguistic features with which our young learners must become familiar. We can easily teach and reinforce the features pertaining to digital text by working with small groups of students using a smartboard in the classroom or with a classroom computer or tablets.

However, there are other ways we can emphasize linguistic features found in printed texts. First we must ensure that the texts contain a variety of linguistic features to prepare K–3 learners for the informational text that they might encounter in the future. Although it is great to have students recognize a table of contents or a glossary, it is not enough. The Linguistic Features Chart found on page 162 of the Appendix might be used to examine the features included in informational texts. There is an area to write the theme or topic at the top. That way, as we are teaching a specific science or social studies topic, we will know which informational texts might be used to introduce or reinforce the linguistic features.

With our earliest learners, we might want to put the Linguistic Features Chart on a document camera and complete the page together as a class. As we share informational texts each day, we can introduce and reinforce the linguistic features the authors use in the texts. As we examine the features, we can discuss why the authors may have chosen to include the text feature and how it can help readers understand the content.

Our slightly older learners, or those students who possess more advanced literacy skills, may be able to go on a scavenger hunt for features with a small group of peers. Give each small group a copy of the features chart to use while looking through texts to locate some of the features. Students write the title of the books and the page number on which a feature is found, so they can share their findings with their classmates. Although not every feature will be found in all texts, by having students complete the chart we will know if there are specific linguistic features to which they are not being exposed. Included on the chart are features that are found in digital texts such as hyperlinks and electronic menus. There are blank rows to list other features that may be found in texts.

The ELA CCSS acknowledge the important role that the linguistic features play in the comprehension of informational text. In fact, beginning in first grade, it is expected that students are able to use the various text features to locate key facts or information (RI.1.5 and RI.2.5). The expectations increase from there. By the time our young learners are in third grade, they are expected to be able to synthesize information found in illustrations and words within the text to demonstrate an understanding of the text (RI.3.7). By introducing these linguistic features at a very early age, we will ensure that our K–3 students will become familiar with them. Students will then be able to build upon their knowledge of the features so that they can use the information provided by the features to enhance their understanding of text.

Types of Informational Text We Might Find in the Classroom

Informational text can be found in several formats in our classrooms. It might be in traditional printed format or it might be digital text found on various technological devices. In addition, students can create informational local text, which can be displayed in the classroom and school. All three types of informational text are important to include in the classroom.

Printed Texts

When we hear the word *text*, traditional printed text is often what comes to mind. These are the texts students hold in their hands and flip through. Many of us still love the look, smell, and feel of a new book. Although technology is changing the way students view texts, I believe that the traditional printed texts will continue to play an important role in classrooms.

The problem with printed text is that it is not realistic for teachers to buy large quantities for their classroom. Further, the school library may not have the quantity or quality of texts we need on a particular topic or theme. One elementary school I visited in Texas years ago allowed its first-grade teachers to determine whether they wanted to purchase the classroom basal series or use the funds that would be spent on those books for children's literature. Those teachers who chose children's literature were able to purchase and use several sets of wonderful texts. They then shared with other classrooms on their grade level so that many sets of texts could be purchased. While not everyone has that type of opportunity, if the opportunity presents itself it is a great way to obtain a large number of quality texts.

A couple of years later, I saw an entirely different situation in a lower SES, rural town with a population of 700. I can remember driving into town and heading for the elementary school, driving over railroad tracks, and passing pink flamingos dotting many of the yards. The teachers were friendly and welcoming, and I loved my time at the school. However, the many days I spent there over the course of a year opened my eyes to the struggles the teachers and administrator experienced as they tried to meet the needs of the students. The library was exceptionally small in the school, and it opened only on days a retired librarian came in. When I asked about getting texts from a local library, teachers informed me that they had to pay to get a library card in a neighboring town so that they could use the library because they were not residents of that county. What was especially sad about the situation is that if it was that difficult for teachers to find texts, it could only be worse for the parents of the students.

If printed books were in such short supply at the school, I can only imagine how many informational texts were available. When Duke (2000) conducted her research in first-grade classrooms in low-SES schools, she found that with the students "a mean of 1.9% of the time spent with written language (as a whole class) involved informational texts" (p. 219). They not only had much less traditional informational text, but also less informational text displayed in the classroom environment. Later in the chapter we will talk about local text. Creating local text is an easy way to populate our classrooms with informational text, so that there shouldn't be any reason for a lack of such texts.

Digital Texts

Students need to be knowledgeable consumers of digital texts. It is one more type of text in the wide range we need to have available for students. Without knowledge of digital texts, students will not have access to "powerful literacies" necessary to compete in the world (Finn, 1999, p. xi). Using this type of text may be of concern to some of us in the educational field who were born prior to the technology revolution. I find it humorous but accurate that Prensky (2005) aptly refers to us as *digital immigrants*. It really is as though we have traveled to a new land and are trying to learn the language and adjust to the culture. Just as younger children often pick up a second language faster, this appears to be true with technology as well. My hope is that we can learn from each other: Those teachers who are digital natives will continue to help digital immigrants adjust to our new surroundings.

Our K–3 students, who are clearly digital natives, are often much more comfortable using technology. They have grown up in a world that surrounds them with text, images, and sound, and yet that doesn't mean they know how to access information (Considine et al., 2009). Therefore, we must make a commitment to work with our earliest learners so that they are savvy consumers of digital texts. The good news is that 99% of our classrooms are now listed as having Internet access (Kleiner & Farris, 2002), so not only do students have access to the Internet but also, in my experience, more and more elementary students have access to iPads because of funding from large grants.

As Liu (2005) has pointed out, digital texts are read differently from traditional printed text that students encounter. Students have to analyze both text and nontext (e.g., graphics, multimedia, images). According to Kress (1997), when our students examine digital text, they must learn to distinguish between those visuals that are pivotal to the content and those that are there only for aesthetic reasons. Just as with traditional printed text, we must teach students to scrutinize digital texts and not assume everything they read is true and accurate.

Whether we like it or not, many people judge an educational setting by the availability of technology. Technology is a vital part of the classroom, but we need to realize one important fact: "Use of technology does not necessarily mean better teaching. The Internet does not represent an alternative 'better than books'; it signifies an option 'different from books'" (Sutherland-Smith, 2002, p. 668). According to Smolin and Lawless (2003), the way we use technology is key. We do not want to add a technological layer to the classroom by having activities that students previously completed with pencil and paper now be completed on a computer. Instead we want to have a broader vision of the use of technology. For instance, students must be able to synthesize information from many sources to build their understanding of a topic, and technology can assist with that by providing access to multiple sources.

In addition, technology allows students to make powerful connections between topics and texts and builds their content knowledge. Intertextuality is the ability to understand one text based upon knowledge gained from a previous text (Kristeva, 1984). Intertextuality should be an important goal for all K–3 classrooms. Our young students need to understand that there is plenty of information available on a topic. In order to meet the ELA CCSS, our kindergartners and first graders must be able to recognize similarities and differences between two texts on the same topic (RI.K.9; 1.9) while our older students have to be able to compare and contrast multiple texts (RI.2.9; 3.9). Appropriate use of technology can help us to meet these standards.

One thing is certain: We must include digital texts in our classroom. It is the only way our students can become better consumers of the wealth of information available through technology. Even with our earliest learners, we must begin building the literacy skills they need for the 21st century. The ELA CCSS acknowledge the importance of digital texts by stating that students must be able to use text features and search tools such as keywords, sidebars, and hyperlinks to locate information relevant to a given topic efficiently (RI.3.5). In order to meet the standards, not only must we make technology available, but we must also use it wisely to help students develop the necessary literacy skills. By doing so, we can create powerful connections between literacy and the content areas so that students are knowledgeable consumers of digital texts.

Local Texts

As long as many of us can remember, educators have touted the importance of a print-rich environment. Years ago, that meant labeling as many things as possible in the classroom so that students would have exposure to words in their environment. Although a print-rich environment is still important today, there are now more specific guidelines that can help K–3 teachers build one that can best meet students' needs (Maloch, Hoffman, & Patterson, 2004). One term that we often see in the educational literature is *local text*. Local text is "the written texts created or constructed by classroom participants" (p. 130).

Although local text can't take the place of traditional printed texts or digital texts, it can provide another option for expanding the amount of available text in a classroom. As was discussed earlier, Duke's (2000) research showed not only a lack of traditional informational text in low-SES first-grade classrooms, but also less informational text displayed in the classroom environment. Regardless of the socioeconomic status of the classroom, there is no reason for a lack of local text. It is inexpensive to create and easy to tie into the content areas, and it helps students to see the importance of their literacy skills. The following suggestions were created upon examination of the local text guidelines established by Maloch et al. (2004). They have been modified to ensure that informational text is part of the print-rich environment.

First, let's look around the classroom. What types of local text are displayed? Is there a variety of text shown, and is at least 70% of it informational text? Given the importance of informational text, and the fact that, historically, research shows an emphasis on narrative text in the K–3 classrooms, it is my belief that 70% informational text should be a goal. It is also important to note that all students need to see themselves as authors of local text. Although a wide range of literacy levels may be present in the classroom, try to find a way that even the youngest readers and writers can contribute to the local text displayed in the classroom.

If, after you've looked at the classroom, it is evident that there may not be as much informational local text displayed as previously thought, look at other K–3 classrooms. Instead of reinventing the wheel, meet with other teachers to see if there are ideas that you can gain from one another. Even if different topics or themes are being studied, it doesn't mean seeing one type of text won't provide ideas to enhance another classroom's local text.

Take time to examine the traditional printed texts and digital texts currently used in the classroom. Then think about how a piece of local text can be connected to those texts. Perhaps students are seeking out key linguistic features in traditional printed texts about community helpers. They are finding charts and diagrams on the types of community helpers and the role they play in communities. Build on students' new knowledge and encourage them to create charts and diagrams for other types of community helpers.

It is important to reflect on how local text is displayed. Just as we don't appreciate printed or digital texts that are cluttered and hard to follow, we wouldn't want the classroom filled with so much local text that students don't acknowledge it. We want to think about how we can make the best use of our classroom space so that quality, meaningful local text is displayed. Also, because local text is inexpensive to produce, it can be frequently changed. Whereas in the past we might have put up a spring bulletin board that spanned several months, we all realized that before the sun had a chance to fade the paper, most students were no longer acknowledging it. In fact, after a few weeks, students probably walked past it. By changing the local text on a regular basis, students will gain more from the materials.

Informational local text provides an excellent opportunity to create confident literacy learners. By referring to the text and engaging our students with it, we can build their vocabulary and help them to expand their knowledge about text conventions and the types of text. We can reinforce with our early learners the importance of always considering the audience, purpose, and content when we write or create a piece of text. These are valuable skills and knowledge that will serve our K–3 students well as they continue on as lifelong literacy learners.

Meet with other teachers at the same grade level and think about the content area topics that will be taught this year. Discuss the types of local texts that will not only tie to those topics but also engage children in the classroom. Think beyond the types of local text that may have been included in the past and brainstorm a list of local text that might be included this year. Be sure to consider the specific knowledge and skills children will gain from creating each type of local text.

Obtaining Texts

If we don't have adequate informational printed text available for our students, we have to find creative ways to obtain such texts. There are a number of organizations that help libraries obtain books. The Libri Foundation is a nationwide nonprofit organization that donates new, hardcover books to small, rural libraries in the United States. It has a list of texts from which to choose and, according to its website, the list includes quality nonfiction texts. Along with The Libri Foundation, a number of other programs that provide books for our classrooms can be found by searching online under "grants for teachers" and visiting NCTE's Elementary Grants webpage: www.ncte.org/grants/elem.

I think DonorsChoose.org is a fantastic website. Many teachers I know have received funding through the website, and it takes little time to create a request. K–12 public school teachers go to the website and write a short description of the project for which they need funding. These projects might pertain to art, field trips, science, or math, among other areas. There is a specific area where teachers can request funding for books. Donors who help fund the grants are not large corporations. Often the people who support projects on the website are individuals who choose to make a tax-deductible donation. I have noticed a number of retired teachers and librarians who donate through this website.

Donors can post their name and why they chose to fund a specific project. Anyone interested in helping educators can read through the website and determine where they want to donate money. Those who have a special interest can narrow their search so that they view requests only from certain types of schools, teachers, grade levels, or one of several other criteria. Donors may be looking to support early childhood programs, Title I schools, or diverse settings. By including specific information in the project description, you can more easily target specific people who may want to support a project.

Donation requests range from small requests to obtain classroom materials to large sums of money, but the key is that many donors make small donations to fund a project. Teachers state their school, the socioeconomic status of the school, a brief description of why they need funding, and a photo of their classroom. Then, for up to four months, the projects can be listed on the website. The best part is that the website is free for teachers to use, and anyone can be a donor because donations as small as one dollar are accepted.

TRY IT OUT

Go to the NCTE grants website at www.ncte.org/grants/elem or DonorsChoose.org. Skim through examples of grants. Look for the types of grants that people are choosing to fund. Draft a grant. Ask a colleague to review the grant request—an extra set of ears and eyes can help you to construct a winning grant. Then share what you wrote with your principal before submitting your grant. You have nothing to lose and a lot to gain!

An elementary teacher in my graduate class told me about a wonderful arrangement her elementary school has with a local library. The program is called Books to Go. When a teacher at her school needs texts pertaining to a topic, he or she e-mails the library with the topic being studied, and the media specialist organizes a crate of books pertaining to the topic and delivers them to the school.

Although I haven't heard of many schools having an arrangement such as this, it sounds like a great way for schools and local libraries, which are often larger than school libraries, to work together to help students have access to texts. If this type of text-lending program does not exist at your school, it can't hurt to call your local library to ask about starting one. In fact, when this elementary teacher shared the idea in my class, a teacher at another school called her local library. Even though the library had a similar program with day-care centers, its staff said they hadn't thought about working with an elementary school. Now, this teacher's school and her local library have a Books to Go arrangement too.

There are also many free e-books available online. At www .techsupportalert.com/free-books-children, educators can access a list of 200 sites for free children's e-books, and the list is updated regularly. I especially like www.wegivebooks.org, a site created by the Penguin Group and the Pearson Foundation, because of the number of informational texts available. All the e-books on the website are picture books for children up to the age of 10.

It might also be helpful to look for short texts to add to the classroom. Short texts include maps, brochures, and periodicals that can tie into the students' activities and interests. Newspapers have informative articles that can be shared with students. Educational magazines such as *Scholastic News*, *Click*, and *Ranger Rick Jr*, could be obtained through grants and can be another way to boost the amount of printed informational text in the classroom.

Deciding Which Texts to Use in Instruction

Now that we know the types of texts we want to use and have an idea of ways to find them, we need to think about how we will choose which texts to use with our students. Almost everyone with a computer has been on Amazon.com, typed in a few keywords for a book topic in the search bar, and clicked on the Go button. However, the choices on such a website can leave the viewer overwhelmed not only by the number of options but also by the time it takes to find the basic facts about each book. Many of those texts may not meet our classroom needs, but it is often difficult to tell from the information provided. Another option is to focus on award winners, but finding informational texts that have won awards can be difficult as well. Not surprising is Colman's (2007) findings that the children's literature field contains more fiction than nonfiction texts. She believes that this is due, in part, to the fact that nonfiction texts are more expensive and time-consuming to produce because of concern with page layouts. Also, myths still perpetuate within the educational community that children won't like nonfiction, and nonfiction won't hook kids on books.

If any of this causes an uneasy feeling that nonfiction or informational texts are not interesting, take a look at some of the recently published titles. Research conducted by Gill (2009) found that the more recently published nonfiction award-winning books emphasize visuals, are more accurate, and are more engaging than those that come to mind for many people when they hear the term *nonfiction*. In fact, in recent years, there has been an abundance of informational texts published on topics of interest to our early literacy learners. With so many informational books to choose from, finding a quality title that engages students should not be an issue.

Identifying Informational Texts

Identifying quality informational texts takes time. Booklists and award winners are a good place to start but not a final destination. For example, some K–3 teachers like to review the Caldecott Medal winners. However, the Caldecott Medal is given each year for the illustrations in a text. Thus, the texts winning the awards may not be informational texts, and even if they are, the award is not given for the content. Educators can also review the Children's Choices and Teachers' Choices booklists on the International Reading Association website: www.reading.org/Resources/Booklists .aspx. Again, there are many books on these lists, and while the number of informational texts included is growing, many of the texts are narrative.

However, there are several ways to search specifically for award-winning informational texts. Consider the following:

- Orbis Pictus Award (www.ncte.org/awards/orbispictus), presented yearly to the author and illustrator of the most distinguished informational book for children
- Robert F. Sibert Informational Book Medal (www.ala.org/alsc/ awardsgrants/bookmedia/sibertmedal), awarded by the Association for Library Service to Children
- Carter G. Woodson Book Award, (www.socialstudies.org/awards/ woodson), an honor given to social science texts

Along with award winners, another valuable source for informational texts is content area committee–published lists of recommended books. Since 1972, the NCSS and the Children's Book Council (CBC) have reviewed and recommended trade books with social studies themes in

Social Education (www.socialstudies.org/resources/notable). In a similar manner, the NSTA and the CBC compile a list of recommended science trade books for K–12 students, which can serve as a great resource for teachers (www.nsta.org/publications/ostb). This information is available in the NSTA's journals *Science and Children*, *The Science Teacher, and Science Scope*. We can use any of these sources when we need a quality informational text related to a content area.

There is one other way to search for quality informational texts that might make searching a lot less time-consuming, and most teachers I work with are not familiar with it. The Database of Award-Winning Children's Literature (www.dawcl.com), created by a former librarian, contains more than 10,000 records from 112 awards. Visitors can narrow their search of texts by requesting specific award winners, publication year, ethnicity of main character, age and gender of protagonist, historical time period, and suggested age of reader. Therefore, it is possible for a K–3 teacher to search for Orbis Pictus books for the suggested age range of 5- through 8-year-olds. It is also possible to search with a keyword or phrase. With a few clicks, texts that won an award and were written on the topic of weather, seasons, or other content area terms can be accessed. This database is one of the easiest ways for K–3 teachers to develop an initial list of texts to review.

Evaluating Informational Texts

Now that we have options for identifying and locating texts, we need to decide which ones we want to use with our students. There needs to be a way to determine which printed and digital texts are quality texts. One suggestion is to select potential texts from the sources cited prior and then use Table 2 (Altieri, 2011) to examine important qualities of the texts. Use the Content Area Trade Book Evaluation sheet provided on page 163 in the Appendix to further guide you. The guidelines and criteria included on the sheet are based on a variety of sources (Atkinson, Matusevich, & Huber, 2009; Cullinan, 1989; Donovan & Smolkin, 2002; Harvey & Goudvis, 2007; Saul & Dieckman, 2005; Sudol & King, 1996).

If a book does not meet expectations on a criterion, then it would earn a *1*; if the text met expectations, it would earn a *3*; and if it exceeds our expectations, it would earn a *5*. Space is provided on the sheet to list

Table 2. Content Area Trade Book Selection Guidelines

Criterion	What to Look For
Accuracy of content	• Author's experience and background are provided. • Photo credits are included. • References are cited. • Information is current.
Cohesion of ideas	• Words and phrases (e.g., *because, therefore, as a result*) signal within-paragraph connections explicitly. • All ideas belong together as arranged. • Abstract concepts are introduced appropriately (e.g., one at a time, concrete and relevant examples).
Organization and layout	• Text layout according to the table of contents is logical. • Text features (e.g., chapter titles, subheadings, glossary, index, visual aids) serve a purpose. • Text pattern is the one most appropriate.
Specialized vocabulary	• Vocabulary is adequately explained through the text, visuals, or glossary.
Student considerations	• Students have the appropriate background knowledge necessary to digest the text. • Format is appropriate (i.e., page and print size). • Positive gender and racial/ethnic role models are provided. • Will interest students
Teacher goals	• Is useful according to teacher goals (e.g., use, standards)

Note. From *Content Counts! Developing Disciplinary Literacy Skills, K–6* by J.L. Altieri, 2011, Newark, DE: International Reading Association.

outstanding features of the books examined. Let's look at these criteria in detail.

Accuracy of Content

This is one of the most important aspects to consider when selecting texts for our K–3 learners. As Rice (2002) encourages, we must not only assess texts for inaccurate information but also look for omissions. Basically, we are doing what we ask our students to do: We must look at texts with a discriminating eye and not assume that what is printed is accurate. We can review the author information, photo credits, references, and even look at the copyright date. It isn't unusual for authors to list consultants they contacted for content-specific information, so be sure to consider that. Also, with the large number of trade books published each year, there is no reason to use one with outdated information.

Cohesion of Ideas

As we focus on informational text, we will want to examine the types of words and phrases that connect the ideas. Are transition words and phrases such as *because*, *therefore*, and *as a result* used to help students follow the flow of the text? Are concepts introduced in a concrete manner with examples so that our young learners understand the content?

Organization and Layout

Examine the illustrations, photographs, graphics (e.g., diagrams, tables), and words. Books that engage the reader with an appealing visual presentation are valuable. Can our K–3 learners relate to the visuals, and are they shown from a child's perspective? Part of the organization and layout includes examining chapter headings, subheadings, glossary, and other linguistic features. We want to have excellent examples to help start our students' journey with informational text.

Specialized Vocabulary

How are vocabulary terms introduced to the reader? Will our students be able to use the context, visuals, or glossary to determine the meaning of unfamiliar terms? We want to begin building our students' vocabulary through the introduction of new technical terms, but we don't want the vocabulary in the text to overwhelm and frustrate our early literacy learners.

Student Considerations

This category is more static that the other criteria. Our students' interests and abilities are changing at an unprecedented rate in the early grades. We can, however, think about whether the topic is presented in a manner that will create even more interest with our students. Also, given that we are working with very young students, we can look at the level of detail included. The same broad topic may be used with K–6 students, but we would not necessarily need that level of detail for students in the primary grades. Also, we want to ensure that there are positive gender and racial or ethnic role models in the text. This requires examining both visuals and words. A study completed years ago by Daisey (1994) shows that minorities and women were absent from or poorly represented in science textbooks. The results of this study should serve as a reminder that we always have to examine the portrayal of people represented in our texts. As teachers of very young students, we have a responsibility to ensure that they see all people portrayed in a positive manner in content area trade books.

Teacher Goals

Finally, let's think about the content of the text and the goals for the lesson. This is a good time to think about the ELA CCSS we want to develop through our classroom activities. Is the text going to help achieve those goals? While each of the other criteria is important, we cannot ignore our own reasons for using a text. If the text can't help us to create those powerful connections we are trying to make, then perhaps we should consider another text.

The purpose of Table 2 is to help eliminate the emotional appeal that is frequently present when we select texts. It is hard not to let certain books grab our attention, so that we can't wait to share them with our young students. However, because of the time constraints already in place in the educational setting, we need to ensure that what we share contains the characteristics of quality informational texts. It will be even more beneficial to complete the Content Area Trade Book Evaluation sheet with colleagues.

What we also need is a quick way to determine whether a text might warrant a closer look later or a way to select a text when time is crunched and it isn't realistic to sit down and examine books. In an ideal world, we would have both the time and resources to meet with other teachers and analyze every text we locate. Of course, we don't live in an ideal world.

We all remember, and some of us still use, the five-finger method for helping students determine if a text is one they might be able to read. The method is popular for many reasons and is a quick and simple concept for students to employ. Well, we can also use a five-finger method as teachers to determine if an informational text is one we might want to share with our students. We just have to remember the five-letter acronym *USE IT*:

Use—Why are we considering the text? What are our goals? What is our purpose? With limited time in the classroom, we need to have a reason for selecting a text. While some texts might grab our eye or be readily accessible, we have to look closely at what we want to accomplish with the text and the ELA CCSS we want to target.

Students—What are our students' interests? What type of experiences do our students have with the type of text or the content presented? Because we work with K–3 students, we have to be cognizant of what experiences they may or may not have had in the past in order to reap the full benefits of the text. Even if students have limited experiences with the type of text or minimal background knowledge, that doesn't mean the text won't work; we just have to spend more time determining how we can develop background knowledge or provide the appropriate context to help our students make connections with the text.

Expertise—When I think about the word *expertise*, I often ask myself, Does the author have any business writing this text? Sure, we can find beautiful colorful photographs in books about plants and animals, but is the content in the text accurate? Look for information in the book that discusses the author's expertise on the topic. Are there photo credits? Are references cited? Most important, is the information current?

Ideas presented—Does the text read well? Does the writing flow? Are there visuals that add information to the words? Are the ideas presented in a way that young children can readily access? For instance, a thick text with small print and black-and-white graphic aids probably isn't the best choice for our early learners. Also, are there subliminal messages being sent through the visuals and words about diversity? We want the ideas presented to include positive portrayals of all people.

Total picture—What are our final thoughts on this printed, digital, or local text? Will it grab the students' interest? Does it meet our goals? Is the information accurate and presented in an interesting manner? If we give it a thumbs up, then we use it. If we don't, we move on.

By using this evaluation method, we might still end up with printed text and digital texts we decide later aren't meeting our needs. That is fine. Just remember that we are surrounded by texts, and we can always replace texts to find those that better meet our needs. With many texts readily available, there is no reason to continue to use a book that doesn't work. Instead, we can look at five key features of books and make a decision whether to *USE IT*.

The Role of Materials in the Classroom Context

Nobody will argue whether the teacher and students are integral parts of any learning environment, but the role of materials is receiving a greater emphasis. Of course, the materials are only as valuable as the way in which they are used. Without a teacher using the texts to create powerful connections within the various content areas, the materials are irrelevant.

As part of this, we need to realize the importance of semantics. When we share stories or poems in the classroom, we need to use the appropriate terms so students recognize that they are stories and poems (RL.K.5), and when we use informational text we need to do the same and use appropriate terms. Photographs, illustrations, and charts are three different types of visuals, and we can help our early learners by differentiating among the various elements of printed text through our word choice. By first grade (RL.1.5), students are expected to be able to explain the differences between stories and texts that provide information. Plays consist of scenes, poetry consists of stanzas, and stories and informational text often consist of chapters. By using appropriate terminology with even the youngest learners, our third graders will be able to refer to the elements correctly, which is expected in the ELA CCSS (RL.3.5).

Our knowledge of materials can serve to build a stable foundation for our K–3 learners. The goal is not to allow texts to replace hands-on science experiments or field trips because our young children need and deserve a broad range of experiences. However, we can use the texts to reinforce and extend the content area learning they are experiencing. We can use texts effectively so that our passive listeners become active, engaged learners. Through rich experiences with texts, students will become more confident in their use of texts and build their information base. Furthermore, through the use of quality informational texts, we can reach our goal of developing content knowledgeable students with strong literacy skills (Reutzel et al., 2005).

REFLECTING BACK AS WE MOVE FORWARD

Text has never played a more important role in the classroom. This is evident throughout the ELA CCSS. In the past, we might have chosen to help our young learners access the information in the text through other modalities instead of attempting to engage them with the text. We now realize how vital it is for all students to encounter a variety of text within the classroom. It isn't an either–or situation, where young children either complete a classroom experiment with plants or read about the stages of plants. Instead, we can help students make the connection by first having the hands-on experience and then using an informational text to show how they might record what they saw and experienced. We might draw our students' attention to the linguistic features in the text and suggest that they use some when they think about a caption as they draw the plant on a sheet of paper or complete a science log.

It isn't enough for students to be able to read a specific content area text. They must develop essential literacy skills so that they access new texts they will encounter in upper grade levels and later in life. This is the only way that students' knowledge base can continue to grow. In the remaining chapters, we will look closely at how we can take our understanding of quality materials and build the type of knowledge and skills necessary for this to translate to lifelong learning for our K–3 learners.

CHAPTER 3

Creating a Strong Foundation

We know the importance of building a strong literacy foundation for our students. In fact, if I asked early childhood teachers to list specific literacy skills they would like students to develop before they walk out of the classroom at the end of the year, I'd bet that knowing the letters of the alphabet, understanding concepts of print, recognizing rhyming words, and reading high-frequency words would be near the top of many teachers' lists.

Rethinking How We View Foundational Literacy Skills

Have you opened the printed version of the ELA CCSS or looked for the foundational skills section on www.corestandards.org? Were your eyes automatically drawn to the beginning of the standards document, right after the introduction and anchor standards? I think a lot of us expect to find the foundational skills listed at the front of the ELA CCSS. In most texts focusing on elementary reading skills, foundational skills would be at the beginning (Psst!: Even I put this chapter near the beginning of this text immediately after the chapter on materials.). That is because many of us have believed for years that foundational skills are where we begin with early literacy learners, and then we proceed to reading comprehension and beyond. However, that is not where we find foundational skills in the ELA CCSS document. The Foundational Skills are in their own section preceded by Reading: Informational Text and followed by Writing. Although that may seem puzzling to us at first, it may help us rethink how we view foundational literacy skills.

Just the word itself, *foundation*, conjures up an image of a base or a strong support on which other literacy levels can be built, but is that always the case? Obviously, in the K–3 grade levels we need to ensure that our students develop these necessary and valuable foundational skills, but to some extent *all* elementary teachers need to teach or reinforce them.

A "vaccination approach" (Shanahan & Barr, 1995) will not work. Basically, *vaccination approach* means exactly what the term sounds like. Those in the medical profession conduct research for years to create a vaccine to eliminate a disease. After the vaccine is created, it is then administered. Children can go to the doctor and get a vaccine for a disease (or condition), and they never have to worry about encountering it again. Over the years, people have assumed that the vaccination approach will work for building literacy skills too.

Literacy learning is more complex than that. As educators, we are working with children who come to us with a variety of experiences, knowledge, and needs. Those of us who have been in the education field for a long time know there is no quick fix to literacy difficulties. When Shanahan and Barr (1995) use the term *vaccination approach*, they are referring to the idea that the educational field often focuses on literacy issues in elementary grades and assumes that when the children are older they will be ready to meet the continuing literacy demands. Research has already shown us that the vaccination approach doesn't work for developing literacy skills. Likewise, foundational skills cannot be developed through a vaccination approach with our youngest students. We can't focus on foundational skills in kindergarten and assume that students can work on other literacy demands in the upper elementary grades.

As teachers of early literacy learners, we cannot provide a solid literacy foundation for our young learners and then expect the rest of their literacy growth to occur. By embedding the foundational skills closer to the center of the ELA CCSS, we are perhaps reminded that, similar to other literacy skills such as reading and writing, the early grades should not be thought of as an ending point for foundational skills. For example, focus remains on phonics, word recognition, and fluency throughout grades K–5 in the ELA CCSS. In Chapter 1, we explained Shanahan and Shanahan's (2008) three-tiered model for skill development and emphasized the importance of refocusing our literacy activities. We can't focus only on foundational skills at the beginning of children's formal education—we must work on enhancing writing to learn, strengthening technical vocabulary, and many other literacy skills.

In an emergent literacy classroom, we see writing, reading, phonics, and other skills intertwined. Conversely, in a classroom taught from a reading readiness perspective, which we hopefully are seeing less and less of in schools, there would be more of an isolated focus on letters, phonics, and other foundational skills prior to developing other aspects of literacy. As stated in the ELA CCSS Foundational Skills introduction, "These foundational skills are not an end in and of themselves; rather, they are necessary and important components of an effective, comprehensive reading program...."

When we look closely at the ELA CCSS, there are important details to note about the foundational skill requirements listed at the various grade levels within K–3. First, the four components (i.e., print concepts, phonological awareness, phonics and word recognition, fluency) mentioned are not consistent across all grade levels. Kindergarten and first-grade teachers are expected to focus on print concepts, phonological awareness, phonics and word recognition, and fluency. However, after first grade, print concepts and phonological awareness are no longer listed as part of the ELA CCSS. It is expected that after first grade, students will have mastered those basic skills and the literacy focus can shift to phonics and word recognition and fluency.

Also, it is worthwhile to remember that even though we may be targeting specific skills with an activity, we may be rewarded with growth in other aspects of foundational skills. For example, Martinez, Roser, and Strecker (1999) noticed that young students who performed repeated readings through Readers Theatre made much greater gains in their reading rate than another group of students even though the goal for the activity was to improve reading expression and not rate. If we watch for teachable moments and look beyond the skills we are targeting, we will be rewarded with seeing much greater literacy growth in our K–3 students.

Differentiating Our Instruction

It is essential that we determine what students already know and differentiate our instruction to meet the students at their current level of knowledge. The ELA CCSS emphasize the importance of differentiating instruction. All students in a classroom will not need to be presented with the same task, and all students will not need to be working on the same skills for a specified period of time. I think Yopp and Yopp (2000) sum it up best when they state, "It is the *quality* of instruction and the *responsiveness* of the instruction to the individuals in the classroom that should have greater consideration than the amount of time" (p. 134). Although Yopp and Yopp are referring to the amount of classroom time spent on phonemic awareness, this statement can apply to any of the foundational skills.

As we think about differentiating instruction, many of us also think about our English learners. Years ago, researchers projected that a large number of English learners would be enrolled in public schools in future years, and now more than 10% of our students are English learners (Garcia, Jensen, & Scribner, 2009). It was not only the classrooms in Florida, Texas, and California that experienced large increases in the number of English learners, but also places many never expected it to occur. From the mid-1990s to the mid-2000s, Minnesota experienced a 137% increase in the number of English learners, and states such as North Carolina and Alabama saw three times as many English learners as previously enrolled (Teale, 2009). We now know that 2.8 million children speak English with difficulty (National Center for Education Statistics [NCES], 2006). Many of these children are currently struggling in our K–3 classrooms.

Kindler (2002) examined state standards for reading in English and found that less than 20% of students who were identified as limited English proficient met state standards. As educators, we must be ready to work with these students to help them become proficient literacy learners. Research has shown that kindergartners who are low SES or Latino/a are at an even greater risk of not developing phonemic awareness and concepts of print (Nichols, Rupley, Rickelman, & Algozzine, 2004). How can we best support their literacy growth?

Of course, differentiating instruction is not limited to working with English learners. We must be prepared to differentiate instruction for proficient students who already possess specific foundational skills so that they are not sitting unchallenged while waiting for other students to catch on to concepts. For example, students who can recognize and name the uppercase and lowercase letters of the alphabet when they enter kindergarten (RF.K.1) do not need to spend extensive amounts of classroom time focusing on that task even if many of their classmates lack that skill. Foundational skills are not meant to be prerequisites to other aspects of literacy, and we must teach reading, writing, speaking, listening, and language concurrently. This not only provides an authentic environment in which to address literacy skills, but it also makes it easier to assess what students know and how best to meet their individual needs. Although ideas will be shared in this chapter for developing the four key components of foundational skills listed for K–3, the amount of time spent on each of the areas will depend on the individual child.

Literacy Growth Inside the Classroom: Reading Readiness vs. Emergent Literacy Environments

We know we have many important standards to teach, and now we have the added pressure of the ELA CCSS reinforcing what our students must be able to do before they leave the primary grades. Therefore, it might make some of us wonder what the ideal classroom environment is for developing these vital skills. Let's look at the morning routine in two kindergarten classrooms.

On a typical Monday in Ms. A's room, students begin the day by meeting on the carpeted area. There they review the month, day of the week, and year. They also talk about the weather and review the schedule for the day. Because Ms. A is aware of the skills that must be taught, she then turns her students' attention to the letter of the week. Students then individually state the name of an object they see in the classroom that begins with the letter. Then they return to their seats and cut pictures from magazines or draw pictures of objects beginning with that letter on a worksheet. These sheets are glued into a Letter of the Week book that takes about 30 weeks to complete because of holidays and field trips. There is just enough time left afterward for students to complete a worksheet. This worksheet requires students to circle the words that are part of the word family /at/. The teaching assistant circulates around the desks to make sure the students understand the task at hand. After the activity is finished, students have free time to play in the dramatic play center or with games in the science center.

Next door in Ms. B's room, students also begin their day with meeting on a carpeted area. During carpet time, Ms. B. asks her students to talk about what they are looking forward to that day. Because it is Monday, many of the students are eager to see how much their plants have grown over the weekend. Together, the class creates a morning message with the date at the top. Students contribute any letters or sounds they know as

Ms. B reads and rereads what they are dictating. The students enjoy helping her to write the message. Then Ms. B focuses on concepts of print as the class chorally reads the message a final time.

Afterward, students work in small groups. One small group meets with Ms. B, and students reread a science poem from the prior week, focusing on fluency. A second group works with the teaching assistant. These students are comparing two texts on plants, one fictional and one informational. A third group of students is busy writing an entry in their science logs about their plant. Some students draw a picture, while others write letters representing the initial sounds they hear in the words and use invented, or temporary, spelling for the remaining part of the words. A few students write a sight word or two on their pages. Ms. B plans to review their entries later to see how students are progressing with phonological awareness.

The differences between the classrooms are obvious. The scenarios represent very different teaching philosophies for early literacy learners. Ms. A clearly believes in reading readiness. Although this philosophy began in the 1920s (Coltheart, 1979), it unfortunately remains a popular philosophy. Ms. B clearly believes in the emergent literacy perspective, which has been supported by research for many years (Connor, Morrison, & Slominski, 2006; MacDonald & Figueredo, 2010) and was brought to our attention by Marie Clay in 1966.

An emergent literacy environment is the best way to develop these early foundational skills in our young learners. Nielsen and Monson (1996) found that children in an emergent literacy kindergarten who were considerably younger than those in the reading readiness kindergarten made greater gains in literacy achievement. In addition, research conducted by Connor et al. (2006) shows that children with weaker emergent literacy skills need more literacy-rich experiences. A class taught by a teacher with an emergent literacy perspective can provide those valuable experiences.

The key difference between a reading readiness classroom and an emergent literacy classroom is the teacher's philosophy. The teacher in a reading readiness classroom plays a significant role in the classroom and imparts information to the students. Those with a reading readiness philosophy believe there is a period prior to being ready to read called *prereading*. During prereading, the teacher must teach specific skills in a specific order so that students are prepared to read. Instead of serving as a facilitator, as one might find in an emergent literacy classroom, the teacher leads the class and teaches skills in an isolated manner. This doesn't allow the flexibility necessary to differentiate instruction for students. In the emergent literacy classroom, the teacher also plays an important role, but the teaching is guided by the students' needs and not dictated by the teacher. That does not mean that skills are not taught in an emergent literacy classroom. As Teale (1984) states, literacy has to be learned. Students cannot master foundational reading skills without a more knowledgeable peer or adult serving as a facilitator who guides them through appropriate literacy experiences.

Literacy materials differ greatly between classrooms led with a reading readiness view or an emergent philosophy view. Because the reading readiness philosophy requires a strict sequence of skills, it makes sense that workbooks play a key role in instruction. When some of that control is relinquished and learning becomes less sequential, it becomes easier to use a variety of texts. This is important because those diverse texts can serve as connections to the content areas. By connecting literacy and the content areas, we are not only creating authentic learning experiences but also are making the most of our limited time in the classroom. Teachers are feeling pressure to develop more and more skills, and time is at a premium.

Activities that occur in emergent literacy and reading readiness classrooms differ. In an emergent literacy classroom, we see K–3 learners writing and reading in science and social studies centers. Students use computers to research and learn more about social studies and science topics instead of using computers for skill-and-drill sessions. There are plenty of collaborative activities to help develop students' oral language.

Although many children come to school with social language, they may lack the instructional language necessary to be successful within our classrooms. According to MacDonald and Figueredo (2010), children are expected to be able to interact in classroom discussions, ask questions about what they are learning, and seek information. For many of our early literacy learners, these skills may not be developed prior to walking in our classroom door. The ELA CCSS include these basic skills in the Speaking and Listening section. Skills such as taking turns, listening to others, asking for clarification, and gaining the floor in a respectful manner to share information are expected to be developed throughout the primary grades (SL.K.1–SL.3.1).

Finally, the physical environments of the two classroom types are different. An emergent literacy classroom has a print-rich environment, including a lot of local text (which was discussed in detail in Chapter 2). It is also unlikely to find letter-of-the-week worksheets in the emergent literacy classroom. For obvious reasons, many in the educational field denounce the practice of the letter of the week (MacDonald & Figueredo, 2010; Wagstaff, 1997). It is a slow process to cover the letters and sounds of the alphabet when you focus on one letter per week. (Did you catch the 30-week time frame when I described Ms. A's room?) Such practice also focuses students' attention on letters and sounds in isolation. When I hear about letter-of-the-week activities, I wonder what happens when Susie moves and attends a different school midyear. What happens when Melvin joins the class 15 weeks into the school year? How do those children catch up?

The materials, activities, and physical environments in a K–3 classroom are all dependent on the teacher's philosophy. Although these are only a few differences between the reading readiness and emergent literacy philosophies, we need to keep the bigger picture in mind. There is a wide range of classrooms. We can't assume that a classroom that is print rich is an emergent literacy classroom. Things are never black and white in educational settings. We have to look at the overall classroom context and see how the teachers and students engage to determine whether we are looking at an emergent literacy or a reading readiness classroom. It is important to keep in mind that students need explicit instruction on foundational skills. Explicit instruction can and does occur in a true emergent literacy classroom. However, *explicit* is not the same as *isolated*. The major difference between a reading readiness and an emergent literacy classroom is that the instruction in an emergent literacy classroom is tailored to meet the students' needs and connects with other learning that is simultaneously occurring.

Take a sheet of paper and fold it in half lengthwise. On the left half, write the words *emergent literacy* at the top. On the top of the right half, write *reading readiness*. Enumerate on the appropriate side of the paper what you do with your students in order to build their foundational skills that may be reflective of each philosophy. Look for patterns. Everyone uses a worksheet from time to time, but using a few worksheets doesn't mean the classroom is taught from a reading readiness point of view. Do you teach writing from the very beginning or wait for reading skills to develop? Think about ways you might modify your teaching to more accurately reflect the type of teacher you would like to be.

Reinforcing Literacy Growth Outside the Classroom

We all are aware of the limited time we have with our K–3 students. We are also aware of the importance of making the home and school connection so that children see the value of their classroom learning in their everyday lives and so their families can be involved with that learning. By making the connection to the world around them, we are helping our K–3 learners view school differently. After all, literacy learning doesn't stop when our students walk out our door at the end of each day.

Many of us struggle with how we can optimize our students' literacy growth outside the classroom. Parents and guardians often want to help, but they don't know how. It isn't enough to share with parents what their children are doing at school. Instead, educators and researchers are finding that caregivers need to be taught specific strategies in order to be effective (Darling & Westberg, 2004). When we have open houses, home visits, meet-the-teacher nights, or conferences, we can help parents and guardians learn to echo read with their children or reinforce the importance of asking questions when the parents orally read their children books. If we are going to take advantage of teachable moments with caregivers, then the activities will need to be simple and easy to use with children.

In fact, Morrow, Kuhn, and Schwanenflugel (2006) found that in order for literacy activities with parents to be successful, the activities need to have three qualities. First, activities have to be simple. They need to be not only easy to understand but also easy to implement with children.

Furthermore, the activities cannot be time-consuming. Many of us have been in the parent role, and we know how overwhelming it can be when a child brings home a project that is time intensive. The project might be finished or it might not. A shortened version might be completed, or it might never be attempted. None of us want to have a child bring in a project that was obviously completed by someone much older.

As teachers, we are constantly trying to find ways to teach more content with less time. Parents are also trying to do more with less time. They are managing a home, providing for their family, and taking care of their most important assets, their children. Although they may want to help their children succeed, it isn't realistic to expect them to have hours of free time on a regular basis to work with their children on a skill. Like us, parents want to see results. Although as teachers, we have become accustomed to waiting to see results, it helps to use activities with parents that provide relatively quick results. If results are not seen, parents may decide that the activity is not worthwhile. Just as children are encouraged when they see progress, so too are their parents or guardians. Realizing that they are making a difference in their children's learning can serve as a motivational device and encourage parents to attempt the next activity the teacher requests. Activities that are simple, quick to implement, and quick to produce results will be the ones most apt to help strengthen children's literacy skills outside of the classroom.

We should encourage parents to use informational texts with their children. Research has shown that when parents and children read informational texts rather than narrative texts, their conversations often involve a higher level of thinking (Price, van Kleeck, & Huberty, 2009). Be aware that it may not be feasible for parents to take their children to the public library—we may need to provide the texts for parents to read. (See Chapter 2 for ways to obtain books for the classroom.) Encourage parents to read other types of informational text to their children as well. Whether parents look at supermarket fliers, newspapers, or magazines, involving their children with texts will not only show that as adults they value literacy skills but also help children to realize the important role that literacy plays in their lives outside of school. The more that children are exposed to informational text, the easier it will be for them to read and understand it.

Brainstorm with your colleagues ideas to actively involve families in developing their children's foundational reading skills. These activities should be simple, be easy to implement, and show results quickly. Try to include informational text in the activities. Then select a few activities that you can share with your students' caregivers to help strengthen the home–school connection. After you have an opportunity to introduce the ideas to parents and guardians and they have a chance to try them out, share results with your colleagues. Were any activities successful? Is there a way some activities might work better with modification?

Four Components of Foundational Literacy Knowledge

Now let's look at the four key components of foundational literacy knowledge discussed in the ELA CCSS so that we can have a better understanding of what each area includes.

Print Concepts (RF.K.1; RF.1.1)

This component is focused on in kindergarten and first grade and includes concepts of print. For example, our youngest learners must understand that we read top to bottom, left to right, and page to page. Students are also expected to know all of the uppercase and lowercase letters of the alphabet. Concept of word is another important skill for students to master. Developing a concept of word involves understanding not only that a word has space both before and after it but also that a word is created through a sequence of letters. In addition, students are expected to understand by the end of first grade that all sentences begin with a capital letter and end with a punctuation mark.

Phonological Awareness (RF.K.2; RF.1.2)

Phonological awareness is another important component of foundational skills. Although some may think that the terms *phonological awareness* and *phonemic awareness* can be used interchangeably, the National

Reading Panel indicates that phonemic awareness is just one aspect of phonological awareness, which is a much broader concept (Shanahan, 2006). Similar to print concepts, phonological awareness skills are focused on in kindergarten and first grade. When referring to standards related to phonological awareness, the ELA CCSS focus on rhyming words, syllabication, onsets and rimes, Consonant-Vowel-Consonant (CVC) letter patterns, and phonemes in single-syllable words. Although many of us have made language play an important part of our early childhood classroom activities, we need to think about the skills we focus on with the activities in order for them to be the most beneficial (Yopp & Yopp, 2000).

With phonological awareness encompassing many skills, how do we know where to begin? There is one key finding that can help guide our planning. Research in the field of literacy has shown us that children often are better able to grasp large units of sound prior to learning smaller units (Stahl & Murray, 1994). I think many of us have focused on phonemes at the beginning of our early learners' literacy process—perhaps we need to rethink that. Therefore, Yopp and Yopp (2000) provide guidelines we may wish to follow when we want to develop phonological awareness in students who may be struggling with the concept. It may be easiest to start developing phonological awareness by focusing on rhyming words. After students master rhyming words, we can help them to understand syllables before focusing on onsets and rimes. Finally, students can focus on phonemes.

Phonics and Word Recognition (RF.K.3; RF.1.3; RF.2.3; RF.3.3)

Phonics and word recognition and fluency are the two key components under Reading: Foundational Skills that are assessed in kindergarten through third grade and beyond. As part of phonics and word recognition, students must demonstrate sophisticated word analysis skills. They must know and be able to decode many vowel and consonant digraph spellings. Along with these sophisticated skills related to vowels and consonants, students are expected, by the end of third grade, not only to recognize high-frequency sight words, but also to decode common prefixes and suffixes (including Latin suffixes).

Phonics and word recognition seems like one component of foundational skills that can easily become isolated instruction without extra attention on our part. This may be because everyone realizes the vast number of vowel and consonant patterns that make up the English language or because there is an overwhelming number of activity books on the market geared toward developing phonic knowledge.

When we are building on phonic knowledge, it is critical to ask ourselves how this activity connects to other literacy learning and to the content areas. Is our end goal for an activity to have our K–3 students be able to state and memorize a rule or learn phonics so that they can become successful readers?

Fluency (RF.K.4; RF.1.4; RF.2.4; RF.3.4)

Fluency is the last of the four components of Reading: Foundational Skills. According to the National Reading Panel report (Shanahan, 2006), fluency has been taught primarily through two approaches: Either students read out loud while the teacher provides explicit assistance, or they are encouraged to independently read silently. As expected, the National Reading Panel did not find that the latter practice, when it was the sole method used, improved student fluency. In the fluency section of the ELA CCSS, young literacy learners are expected to be able to read prose and poetry with both accuracy and fluency. This includes having the appropriate rate and expression. Furthermore, students must demonstrate metacognitive awareness. For students in first through third grades, they must use context to determine if what they are reading makes sense, and they are expected to know when rereading is needed.

Although fluency is the last part of foundational skills discussed in the ELA CCSS, it is no less important than any previous section. Without fluency, our students will never become good readers. In fact, research by Stanovich (1991) has shown us the importance of fluency when predicting reading ability. A lack of fluency can be a reliable predictor of comprehension problems. This makes sense when we examine the three elements of fluency: accuracy, rate, and prosody (or expression).

Individually, each fluency element is meaningless. It is only when the three parts work in tandem that students develop strong literacy skills. It is important to remember that the task we assign our students can create issues for those who struggle with fluency. When we are initially working with struggling readers and are striving for fluency, we need to limit the length of text students are asked to read. Fluency will be an issue if we expect students to read a lengthy text (Best, Floyd, & McNamara, 2008). Let's look at the three elements.

Accuracy

We all know the importance of accuracy with early readers. If students make miscues, or oral deviations from text, and read *horse* instead of *house* and *breakfast* instead of *bright*, we know that meaning will be lost. Our K–3 learners must monitor their comprehension and develop accuracy so that they derive the correct meaning from text. Thus, we have to emphasize accuracy in teaching. However, a student who reads word by word "There (pause) is (pause) a (pause) fire (pause) in (pause) the (pause) house" may have accurate reading, but the reading is so labored and slow that by the end of the sentence, he or she cannot remember words read earlier in the sentence. The ultimate goal of reading—comprehension—is lost. Accuracy is vital, but the accurate reading of words doesn't guarantee that students will comprehend text. We have all worked with word callers who can read any chunk of text they encounter, but their literacy skills end there. They *sound* like great readers, but when a question is asked it is evident that they have no clue what they just read.

Rate

Reading rate, the next element, has always been a concern of mine. Although it is important to develop an adequate rate of reading, I have found that many students, regardless of the grade, see fast reading as *the* best way to read. They think students who read fast are the best readers in the class. Therefore, we have to be cognizant of how we emphasize reading rate. Reading rate must be appropriate so that readers can understand what they read. Students who read too slowly will have comprehension issues because they are fixating on each letter and word and therefore not getting the bigger picture. Students who read too quickly will also not remember what they read. Clearly, developing fluency is a balancing act where we have to carefully weigh the amount of emphasis put on each element. This is especially true with reading rate. We do not want to focus on rate to the exclusion of the other two fluency elements, or our young learners may think good reading is synonymous with fast reading—and we all know that is not true. At the same time, the reading rate should not impede students' understanding of text.

Prosody

Prosody is vital. We have all read sentences that have different meanings depending on how they are read. I have found myself, on rare occasion, reading a newspaper article or an article headline on the Internet and not quite getting the intended meaning of the text because I paused at the incorrect point. That is where prosody comes into play. Students have to know when to pause in a sentence and why end marks are important. The entire meaning of a sentence can change if students are not demonstrating prosody. Reading accurately and fluently is great, but appropriate expression is vital for students to understand text.

So how do we determine if a student has mastered fluency? As Hudson, Lane, and Pullen (2005) point out, "a fluent reader can maintain this performance for long periods of time, can retain the skill after long periods of no practice, and can generalize across texts" (p. 702). All three elements are important and must occur in unison (Gambrell, 2004; Rasinski, 2006). Although some students can read a very short sentence fluently after repeated readings, we would never consider those children to be fluent readers. I think the key is the ability to read fluently without much effort. Clearly, fluency is a vital component of foundational skills, but according to Kame'enui and Simmons (2001) it is often a neglected part of the reading instruction.

Activities for Developing Students' Foundational Literacy Skills

As educators, we realize that all of the foundational skills play a key role in our instruction, and no one component is more important than another. Through authentic reading and writing experiences (not isolated instruction), we can best develop these skills (Griffin & Olson, 1992). Research with English learners also emphasizes the importance of providing meaningful interactions with print (Lenters, 2004). Foundational skills are not prerequisite skills and should be taught along with reading, writing, speaking, listening, and language in a classroom, which fosters emergent literacy development. Within this setting we can easily make powerful content area connections so that students are developing literacy skills in a meaningful way. According to Shanahan and Shanahan (2008), "sound later-reading instruction needs to be built on a solid foundation of sound early-reading instruction if students are going to reach literacy levels that enable them to compete for the most lucrative jobs" (p. 43). We must seek to help students connect all four components of foundational literacy skills in order to build literacy learners capable of disciplinary learning.

All of the activities discussed in this section can be completed in a classroom setting with K–3 learners and are designed to target a variety of foundational skills. Although certain activities may appear to be more appropriate for our younger students, it is often possible to modify those activities to involve older students in the activity. In keeping with the purpose of this text, the goal of each activity discussed is to reinforce content area connections.

Starting the Morning Right

I saw an activity that was similar to this done years ago in a first-grade classroom, and the students eagerly participated and developed a lot of foundational skills at the same time. Times have changed though, and children may no longer see parents reading a newspaper each morning. The updated version, which I am sharing here, can easily help students develop awareness of the diversity of text used in the home and also lead to gaining new knowledge that will help them make content area connections. This activity might be done once a week for a month or one morning a month throughout the year.

How It Works

1. Send home a note with students asking their parents or guardians to send in a piece of text the children might see adults read at home. Suggestions include a newspaper, magazine, or a supermarket advertisement. Inform the parents that their children will be writing on the text.

2. Explain to students that years ago, it was more common for parents to have a cup of juice or coffee and read the daily newspaper. They are going to take part in a similar activity, but they will use whatever type of printed text their parents tend to read in the home.

3. Students vote on the type of drink they might want to have with their morning text (provided there are no allergy restrictions in the classroom).

They might vote on water, milk, juice, or sugar-free hot cocoa. Students can tabulate the results on a large wall graph to see which drink receives the most votes. That is the drink they will enjoy.

4. The morning prior to the activity, collect all the texts sent in from parents, and ensure that all students have something to read. If necessary, have extra newspapers, magazines, and supermarket advertisements available for those students who do not bring a piece of text to class. Let these students select the type of text they are most familiar with outside the classroom context.

5. The day of the activity, allow students to enjoy their beverage and browse through their text. As with classroom manipulatives, students will probably want to just look at the text for a few minutes without specific directions. This is especially true if there are visuals in the text. Then ask the students questions about their text: Why do people read it? What type of information does it contain? Does it have photos or illustrations? Do the texts tie to any of the content areas? Perhaps the supermarket advertisements tie to math because the text has prices listed or maybe the newspaper shows weather charts that tie to science.

6. Have the students circle a boldfaced word or an italicized word in their text. They might also be asked to focus on certain word recognition skills. Perhaps students will search for sight words they are learning or words that belong to a specific word family. The skills covered can be modified depending on the students' grade level.

Listening Musical Chairs

Who doesn't love a good game of musical chairs? In this game, however, there is no music. Instead of moving to music, students move to words. Listening Musical Chairs is a fun way to get students up and moving in the classroom while building their sight word knowledge. It is a great reason to reread a favorite class text.

How It Works

1. Select a text that has been shared before, can be read aloud in one setting, and ties to a content area. It is important to use a previously read

text because students won't engage with it while they are focusing on listening for specific words.

2. As with musical chairs, put out a chair for all but one student in a circle. That one student will sit in a chair outside of the circle. Each student is handed a word card with a specific target word from the text written on it. Students in the circle take turns reading their words aloud to make sure they know the words.

3. Explain the rules to students. Every time a student hears the word on his on her card, the student should get up and walk—not run—around the circle clockwise before returning to his or her seat. If a student hears the word on the card repeated again while walking around the circle, he or she must walk around another time. This rule applies to all students, including the student who is sitting in the chair outside the circle, or the hot seat. When not walking, the students will stay seated.

4. Explain that there will be three "hot" words in the text. These words should occur about one third of the way through the text, two thirds of the way through the text, and then at the end of the text. While students are listening for the individual word on their card, they must also be listening for the hot words. When a hot word is said, anyone who is up walking around the circle should grab the first available chair. The goal is to get a chair in the circle. The only student who will stand up and try to get an empty chair even if already seated is the student sitting outside the circle. Whoever is left without a chair has to sit in the chair outside the circle (the hot seat).

5. Review the rules one more time, and tell the students the first hot word. Then read the first part of the text.

6. Students get up and walk around the circle as they hear their word called. When the hot word is called, anyone standing at the time will try to get the first seat they can get, and the person seated in the hot seat outside the circle will get up (if not already up) and try to get a seat in the circle. Whoever is standing after everyone grabs a seat goes to the hot seat.

7. Give the students the second hot word, which is found about two thirds of the way through the text, and read the next part of the text following step 6.

8. Repeat one final time by giving the last hot word and repeating step 6.

9. After playing the game, put the words on the individual cards up on the document camera or interactive whiteboard and have the class chorally read through the words. See if students can find patterns within the words. Perhaps five or six words end in *–ed* or *–ing*. It may be that several of the words are proper nouns. The goal is to get students rereading and analyzing the words.

Creating Predictable Books

Creating simple predictable books takes little time, and yet the activity provides numerous benefits for students. Students not only develop print concepts, but also build vocabulary knowledge and reinforce content area learning.

How It Works

1. For our youngest learners, consider using symbols for some of the words in the predictable books. Some schools may furnish software programs such as Boardmaker, which is a graphics database that you can use to create symbol reading. There is an online community where teachers can share with other teachers the items they create with Boardmaker. Another program is Widgit Essentials Bundle, which replaced Writing with Symbols 2000. It also allows teachers to make symbol-reading books. Of course, there is nothing wrong with creating symbols the old-fashioned way either by drawing them or taking a photo. The important thing to remember is to keep the symbols simple.

2. Try to tie the content of the predictable books into the content area studied. If students are learning about community helpers, have a symbol for doctor, teacher, postal worker, and others.

3. Place the symbol above the correct word in the sentence. Parents or guardians of English learners may also write the word in the student's native language underneath the English word.

4. Follow the advice of Fountas and Pinnell (1999) for creating books for young learners and write only one line per page. As we read the predictable texts with our students, we want to point to each word as they read.

5. Use the predictable books as opportunities to reinforce print concepts such as left to right, top, bottom, illustrations, photos, and so forth.

Phonemic Linking Game

This activity, which is based on the Bag Game created by Yopp and Yopp (2000), reinforces students' ability to segment phonemes. The ability to segment phonemes is a predictor of future reading ability, and many kindergarten and first-grade teachers focus on that skill. Until students can break a word apart into the smallest units of sound, they will have difficulty trying to write the sounds. Although many teachers use Elkonin boxes, where students move a marker into a box for each sound they hear, the phonemic linking game can be a fun way to reinforce the skill. This is an easy activity to tie to a content area.

How It Works

1. First, decide which content area topic you want to target. Identify 10–20 content area words related to the topic that you would like to reinforce with students. If the topic is the ocean, use words such as *sun*, *sand*, *fish*, *shells*, *picnic*, *bucket*, *water*, and *swim*.

2. Find a small object that represents each word to put in a resealable bag. If you can't find an object, use a picture of the word. (Objects, however, make the activity a lot more interesting for little ones.) Put the number of interlocking cubes needed to represent each sound in the word in the bag. Unifix cubes, snap-lock beads, or anything that interlocks will work.

3. Seal all the bags and put them in a large container. If the theme is the ocean, a beach bag may work well. If you are studying the spring season, perhaps a child's wheelbarrow or a large flower pot can hold the individual bags.

4. Gather the students together and tell them that you know they are learning a lot about the topic. Then tell them they are going to play a sound game on that topic.

5. Have one student reach into the container and pull out a bag. Open the bag and have the student name the object. After naming the object, the student pulls apart one bead or cube at a time as he or she says each sound in the name.

6. Repeat step 5 with the remaining unopened bags.

Additional Suggestions

This activity doesn't have to be limited to phonemic awareness or the ability to segment phonemes. You can also use it to build technical vocabulary as students discuss the objects and how each object relates to the topic. Some students may be ready for a greater challenge and may name the letter or letters that give the initial sound in the object's name.

Scaffolded Writing

Scaffolded Writing (Douville, 2000) is a great way to reinforce concept of word with young children. The beauty of this activity is that it can be used with a wide range of early literacy learners. Instead of having specific expectations for students, we can easily keep copies of scaffolded writing to see signs of improvement with individual students. Research shows that this is an effective strategy for young children, and it not only develops concept of word, but it can also increase the number of phonemes children recognize in each word (Bodrova & Leong, 1998).

How It Works

1. Begin with a shared science or social studies activity. Perhaps students are learning about seasons in science and have just finished collecting leaves from outside.

2. Tell students that they are going to write about that task of collecting leaves. They have to think about their purpose for writing. It may be that they want to tell their parents or guardians who are coming to school for parent night what they are learning or it may be that they want to share with classroom visitors facts about the leaves they collected. Even at the earliest of ages, it is important to reinforce that writing has a purpose. Writing is designed to communicate ideas for a reason. Whether writing is done to entertain, inform, or persuade, we can help our youngest learners think about its purpose.

3. Meet individually with students and ask them to dictate a sentence to you, making a line for each word.

4. Encourage students to write whatever they can on each line. Some may only put a letter while others may put more phonemes. Some students

may *write* several sentences while others may be able to dictate one or two sentences only.

5. Keep copies of what was written so that the writing can serve as a way to monitor writing progress.

Letter to the Class

Although teachers may already use something similar to this strategy to start the day in a K–3 classroom, Letter to the Class is an excellent way to reinforce all the valuable skills that can be gained through purposeful planning. With a little planning, this activity reinforces phonics and word recognition skills and connects with student content area learning.

How It Works

1. Before students arrive each day, write a daily Letter to the Class on chart paper. Display the letter on an easel all day. Be sure the letter includes the date, a greeting, a body, and a closing. Each day begin the letter the same way, such as "Dear 5K, today is_____." From that point on, include a lot of sight words as you tell the students something they will do that day related to content area instruction, ask them questions about something they learned the day before, or introduce a new content area topic. Letter to the Class is a great time to work in a word or two of content area vocabulary. The letter may contain only four sentences, but it should be full of sight words and CVC words.

2. When students arrive, give them a minute to look at the letter. Then read the letter to the students. As they follow along, sweep your finger under the text. When you get to words the students do not know, stop and segment them. Then blend them back together.

3. Once the entire letter is read, have the class reread the letter once or twice for fluency.

4. Next, the students become "letter detectives." To prepare for their search, they should put on their imaginary high-powered binoculars and adjust them so that they can notice everything in the letter.

5. Students can look for high-frequency words, silent-*e* words, naughty *y*-words (where the *y* takes the place of a vowel), frequently occurring affixes, and compound words (as the year progresses). Circle, underline, or

draw boxes around all the concepts that the students have been learning and are recognizing.

6. Now it is time to assemble the "punctuation patrol." Students must find and identify the punctuation marks in the letter.

7. Write punctuation marks on a stack of sticky notes and then use them to cover up the punctuation marks in the letter. The goal is to place a sticky note with a punctuation mark different from the punctuation mark the sticky note covers up. Let the students try reading some of the sentences with new punctuation marks, and talk about how it changes the sentences. Along with students finding the sentences pretty funny, the activity will reinforce the importance and meaning of punctuation marks.

8. End the activity by having the whole class do one final choral rereading of the text because by now students can read it in its entirety.

9. Select one student each day to take the Letter to the Class home to share with family members.

A Look Inside One Classroom
One kindergarten teacher writes a Letter to the Class each morning. Figure 2 is an example of one of her daily Letters to the Class.

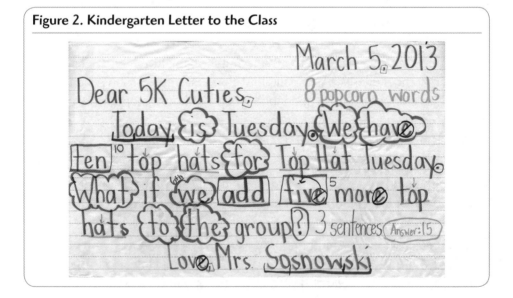

Figure 2. Kindergarten Letter to the Class

Along with reviewing sight words, or popcorn words, the silent *e*, and the bossy *e* (when the letter *e* makes the vowel say its name), the teacher was able to work in quite a bit of information about math. Because the kindergartners were starting to make the transition to using the word *add* instead of *and* for math problems, the teacher included a math problem in the Letter to the Class with the word *add* in it. After circling their popcorn words, students reviewed their ordinal numbers by counting to the sixth popcorn word and marking it. They also counted the number of sentences. Then the students found the two numbers that were spelled out in the problem and wrote the numeral that corresponded with each number word. The students decided the keywords were the two number words and the word *add* and put a rectangle around those three words. As the class read the letter again, the teacher pointed out that math problems often have a question and an answer. Then it was time to figure out the answer to the problem, and 10 kindergarten students wearing paper top hats stood up. Five children joined them. They figured out the answer to the math problem was 15.

For the Birds

This strategy appeals to students' interest in technology and videos. It can serve to reinforce phonic knowledge as the students dictate the dialogue to you or attempt to write it themselves. In addition, the activity reinforces the importance of punctuation. Without paying attention to punctuation, it is impossible for students to read fluently because they will miss the meaning of the text.

How It Works

1. Review various punctuation marks. Talk about why each punctuation mark is used and the importance of using the correct punctuation marks at the appropriate times.

2. Show the students a short film such as the animated film *For the Birds*. It lasts about three minutes, and it won an Academy Award for Best Animated Short Film in 2001. The film can be accessed for free here: onlineshortfilms.net/watch/for-the-birds-video_a66bc019b.html. However, any age-appropriate short film that has a lot of action but no words will work for this activity.

3. After students have watched the entire film, discuss what was occurring in it. If students have difficulty understanding or discussing the sequence of events, replay the film, pausing at 30-second increments.

4. Then replay the film, pausing at five or more points. Ask the students to create the dialogue that they think is occurring in those places. You will want to note where you paused the film so that you can replay it later, stopping at the same points.

5. As the dialogue is written on the board, have students determine which punctuation marks might be used. (Third graders may be able to write their own dialogue.) If students are unsure which punctuation mark is best, write the dialogue with various punctuation marks and read the dialogue expressed with each punctuation mark.

6. Once students have written or dictated dialogue for each stopping point, replay the film, pausing at each point to have a student read the written dialogue for that point. Students will enjoy the activity and have an opportunity to work on their use of punctuation marks.

PWIM
. . . .

PWIM, or Picture Word Inductive Model, was developed by Emily Calhoun in 1999. You can use the activity with small groups or an entire class. PWIM can help students notice phonetic principles of words and expand their sight word knowledge. Many young children have a rather wide range of words in their speaking and listening vocabularies, and this strategy seeks to get those words into their writing and reading vocabularies. PWIM can also easily connect to the content areas being studied at the lower elementary grades.

How It Works

1. Select an illustration, photograph, or some other type of picture that represents a content area topic the class will be discussing. Make a large copy of the visual that can be put on chart paper or the smartboard. Be sure that all students are able to see the picture and that you are able to write on it. If the class is discussing habitats in science, the visual might be a photo of the ocean. If you are studying plants, then it might be an illustration of a large greenhouse and nursery.

2. Ask students to tell you what they see in the picture. This is an important part of the process because students are learning from other students' oral vocabularies. Facilitate the discussion as necessary by asking questions. As the students provide you with words, draw a line and write the word. You can ask for help spelling the words (e.g., What is the first sound you hear in *leaves*? The /sh/ sound in *fish* is similar to a word we talked about last week, *ship*. Does anyone remember what makes that sound?). After the words are written, take the opportunity to repeat words while running your hand under the letters.

3. Read and review everything the class wrote. As you read each word, have the students repeat after you.

4. Decide if there are any words that students might want to add.

5. Talk about why titles are used for pictures and chapters in texts. Reinforce that titles are often short. Brainstorm ideas that might make a good title for the picture. Get suggestions from the students and then write the title on the chart.

6. Draw students' attention to the words. Are there any interesting patterns or sounds the words have in common? What students mention will vary depending on what is in the picture and their oral vocabularies. However, use this teachable moment to reinforce some of the phonic knowledge they have been learning.

7. See if any of the students can take a word from the chart and create a sentence using the word.

8. Help the students take the sentences and create a class paragraph.

9. Read through the paragraph.

10. Leave the chart up in the classroom. Students can revisit it as the unit progresses and continue to build on their vocabulary. They may even decide that some words they used could be replaced with more precise words. (For example, they may decide that the term *flower* is not specific enough for one item in the picture because they now know that it is a tulip.)

A Look Inside One Classroom

A second-grade teacher chose to use this strategy while teaching a unit on continents. During this social studies unit, the class learned about many continents. In order to build background knowledge for each continent, the class participated in read-alouds of informational texts tied to the geographical areas. For the picture part of the strategy, the teacher used a large, colorful map and wrote student-dictated words and phrases directly on the map. The students continued to refer to the map as they added information that they were learning about other continents. The map is shown in Figure 3.

As students gave suggestions for words related to a continent they studied, the teacher provided scaffolding and asked them for assistance with spelling words on the map. The students also looked at patterns in other words they had written in order to spell new words. Once the teacher was comfortable that the students had the terms in their oral vocabulary, the students dictated a collaborative text that the teacher wrote on the document camera. This provided reinforcement, as the terms were used in context and spelled again. The next day, the students reviewed

Figure 3. PWIM Map

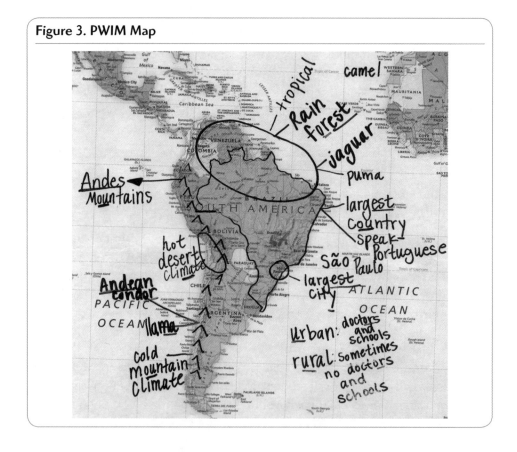

the information and then took their knowledge and added pages to an individual book on continents they were each making. Each continent had a page on climate, people and culture, and animals. (The class lessons on South America will be discussed in detail in Chapter 5 because the teacher chose to use the Tagxedo activity as part of the writing activities tied to South America.)

Through this activity, the second-grade teacher was able to reinforce the students' use of phonics while building their content area vocabulary. She also provided the students with additional experience with viewing maps, fostered discussion with an oral reading of informational texts that tied to the topic, and enhanced their writing to learn skills through the collaborative text and the individual texts. The teacher felt that the students' spelling demonstrated on individual texts was much better than they displayed with other activities. Not only were the students learning to write content area vocabulary words such as *rain forest*, *climate*, and *desert*, but also they were fostering their use of phonics and word recognition skills as they analyzed different words they wrote and worked together to determine sounds they heard in the various words.

Going on a Trip

This activity is based on Yopp and Yopp's (2000) Hungry Thing activity. This activity not only provides another opportunity to read aloud and discuss a text, but also is a great way to get young children playing with words. What better way to build word consciousness or an interest and awareness in words? The activity involves rhyming words, making predictions, and identifying initial sounds in words.

How It Works

1. (This step can be skipped if necessary.) Tell students that you are going to share a story about a very funny creature. If possible, obtain a copy of one of Slepian and Seidler's books about the Hungry Thing (*The Hungry Thing* [1967/2001], *The Hungry Thing Returns* [1990/1993], or *The Hungry Thing Goes to a Restaurant* [1993]). Although these phenomenal books are out of print, there are options for purchasing used copies rather inexpensively from various Internet retailers. The price varies widely between the books and sites. Each of these stories is about a creature and,

on occasion, his sidekick, a small hungry thing. Both things want food, but they can't quite get the words correct. They ask for flamburgers, bellyjeans, tickles, and other foods. If you can obtain a book, read the story and let students make predictions about what foods they think the creatures really want to eat.

2. If you cannot obtain copies of any of the Hungry Thing books, begin by telling students that a very funny creature, the Hungry Thing, decided to visit the classroom last night. Prepare in advance a large cardboard cutout of the Hungry Thing with a "Help" sign hanging around his neck. Of course, the Hungry Thing did not come alone—he brought a suitcase with him and a note for the class! According to the note, the Hungry Thing is going on a flip with the suitcase. Ask students if they think he is really going on a flip. Where do people usually take suitcases? Yes, on a trip! The Hungry Thing needs students' help. He mixes up the letters and sounds in his words. There is a huge list of items that he wants to pack for his trip, but the students will have to come up with the correct rhyming word for each nonsense word in order to figure out what the Hungry Thing wants to take.

3. Ask the students if they think they should unlock the Hungry Thing's suitcase. What do they think is inside? When it is opened, the students will find word cards that have the nonsense words written on them and magazine or clip art pictures of each item.

4. Read each nonsense word and see if students can come up with the correct item the Hungry Thing wants to take with him. As a class, write out the correct word on the card, and then allow one student to find the matching picture of the object in the suitcase to glue on the card.

5. Review the nonsense and real words one more time as each student drops his or her card into the Hungry Thing's suitcase.

6. Hand out brown paper bags, washable markers, and paper. Let the students create their own backpacks filled with items they might want to take to grandma's house, to school, or on a trip.

7. Then the students can share with the class or a partner the contents of their backpack. Each student tells a partner where he or she is taking the backpack. Then the student can tell his or her partner what is in the backpack. If the student says, "I want to take my backpack to school, and I have a brand new *krencil*," the partner must figure out he or she means

pencil. Allow one student to share each of the items in the backpack, and then repeat the exercise with the other partner.

8. Put the Hungry Thing's suitcase in a center and fill it with objects related to a trip to the ocean, the mountains, or another place. Encourage the students to play with the suitcase and come up with nonsense words for each of the items.

REFLECTING BACK AS WE MOVE FORWARD

Foundational skills have always been an important component of K–3 classroom instruction and will continue to be. The ELA CCSS reinforce the importance of such skills with a section of standards dedicated to the foundational knowledge children should possess. As we teach and reinforce these skills, we can also use the activities to help our students make powerful connections that will extend into the content areas they are studying. As we reflect back on our teaching of foundational skills, we must ensure that we are explicitly teaching the skills without isolating the skills. We must also try to develop all aspects of literacy instruction while we target these skills. In that way, we can move our students forward so that they are ready for the disciplinary demands they will continue to encounter in the content areas.

CHAPTER 4

Challenging Our Students With Text

An aspect of the ELA CCSS that has prompted an incredible amount of discussion is the emphasis on complex text. Within the sections Reading: Literature and Reading: Informational Texts, there are standards listed for Range of Reading and Level of Text Complexity. It isn't surprising that the issue of text complexity is spurring such debate. Many of us have been taught for years that there are three levels of text: frustration, instructional, and independent. We were taught to administer individual informal reading inventories so that we could determine what grade level material is instructional level for each student. Instructional-level text was believed to be the level that students were expected to be able to read with assistance. In fact, we were cautioned not to use text that was too challenging lest the students struggle and to provide independent-level text when students were reading on their own at home or in free time. Although informal reading inventories can provide a wealth of information, we are now rethinking exactly what level of text we should be using with our students.

In the past, I think many of us erred on the side of caution and, for many students in the higher grade levels, high-interest, low-readability texts became popular. By using high-interest, low-readability texts, many in the educational community believed that struggling students developed confidence in their ability to read, found interesting topics for their ability level, and could actually read the text. This would be fine if our students didn't need to read anything beyond newspapers and magazines in their lives. In fact, many educators and researchers (e.g., Shanahan, Fisher, & Frey, 2012) now believe that reading easier text isn't adequately preparing students for the future. Students who aren't challenged with text will not be able to handle the content area demands they will encounter in future grade levels and the types of reading that is required in many careers. In order for students to be successful in life and to become contributing members of society, they must engage with complex text.

I look back on my first year of teaching. My first graders could not handle the social studies texts, or so I believed. Educators in the field encouraged me to put the texts away and teach the students through other modalities, such as audiotapes, which were popular resources to help struggling readers at that time. Although that was years ago, I have met many primary-grade teachers who still prefer to teach through other modalities if the text is a challenge for students. With the ELA CCSS demanding that elementary students at second grade and above be able to independently read and reflect on complex text, we can't put the challenging books we have in a closet. We have to find a way to engage our youngest learners with these texts in order to prepare them for more complex texts in the future. Our K–1 students should not be expected to read independently from challenging text, but that doesn't mean that they can't be introduced to such texts.

Of course, we don't want to use only complex texts with our students. According to Standard 10 of the ELA CCSS, students in K–5 need to experience stories, dramas, poetry, and informational text. As teachers, a lot is expected of us. We need to determine the complexity of texts used in our classroom, ensure that our students have the opportunity to experience texts representing a wide variety of genres, topics, and difficulty levels, and know how to motivate and support our K–3 learners as they engage with the complex texts.

What Makes a Text Complex?

This seems to be the million-dollar question right now. To help answer it, Appendix A of the ELA CCSS suggests three areas to examine: quantitative dimensions, qualitative dimensions, and task and reader considerations.

Quantitative dimensions factor in word frequency, sentence length, and text cohension (to name a few). There are numerous quantitative measures listed in Appendix A that are used to determine a text level. Many teachers already know how to determine the level of a book through quantitative measures, and I often hear discussions about Lexiles. Therefore, this aspect of text complexity is not hard to determine, but the issue is that quantitative measures represent only one component of text complexity, and we all realize the limitations of formulas.

Qualitative dimensions are more subjective than quantitative dimensions. Although the qualitative dimensions are categorized into four groups (structure, language conventionality and clarity, knowledge demands, and levels of mean or purpose) in the ELA CCSS, reality is that practitioners and researchers are continuing to grapple with this area. These are very broad areas to take into consideration.

The final aspect to consider, according to the ELA CCSS, is the reader, the task, and the role of the teacher. Paratore (2011) suggests that the instruction from the teacher is what needs to differ. Many of us have read the seminal studies conducted by Richard Allington in the 1980s. I still remember the "a-ha!" moment I had as I read an article he wrote about reading groups. I was teaching third grade at the time, and the article struck home. I was doing what research showed many teachers were doing at the time. My struggling readers were not getting the same instruction as my good readers.

Allington's (1984) research with early learners showed us that poor readers were reading a lot fewer words during the time allotted for reading groups and, unlike the better readers, their time was focused more on decoding and reading aloud than comprehension. Teaching like this also contributes to what Stanovich (1986) refers to as the "Matthew Effect" in reading: The rich get richer, and the poor get poorer, so we see a widening gap between good and poor readers as schooling progresses. Although this research occurred more than 20 years ago, it continues to serve as a reminder that the most important variable in the classroom is the power of the teacher. Few people believe that text difficulty lies solely within the printed symbols on the page. It is what we do with that text that serves either to help or to hinder our young literacy learners. We must differentiate our instruction to help all students understand complex text.

Analyzing Text Complexity

Many researchers and practitioners are trying to determine what influences text complexity. In fact, Fisher, Frey, and Lapp (2012) have identified 13 factors that they believe influence the difficulty of a text. White (2012) details 34 characteristics of texts that could either make text easier or more confusing for adolescents and adults. After reviewing their suggestions and considering the texts often encountered by early learners, I have created a Text Complexity Chart that you can use when examining the texts in K–3 classrooms. Table 3 contains a set of guidelines that you might consider when evaluating the texts we use to make powerful connections in the content areas. It is based on criteria and suggestions from a variety of sources (Fisher et al., 2012; Shanahan & Shanahan, 2008; White, 2012). Although Table 3 isn't inclusive for every factor that might influence text complexity, it addresses many factors that can confuse K–3 learners when they are reading. I wanted to make the information in the table practical, relatively easy to understand, and something that teachers could use to guide their thinking about text.

The Text Complexity Chart, provided on page 164 of the Appendix, can be used to list and analyze texts chosen for a particular theme or topic. Figure 4 shows a complete sample chart. The ELA CCSS encourages "blurring the lines between content areas." Standard 10 emphasizes the importance of texts being "selected around topics or themes that systematically develop the knowledge base of students." Standard 10 further states that "Within a grade level, there should be an adequate number of titles on a single topic that would allow children to study that topic for a sustained period." Although there is room for only three texts to be evaluated on each Text Complexity Chart, it is expected that

Table 3. Factors Influencing Text Complexity

Criterion	Examples	What to Look For
Ease of language	• Figurative language	• Metaphors, similes, idioms
	• Word choice	• Glossary for technical words
		• Multimeaning words
		• Polysyllabic words containing morphemes
Presentation of information	• Linguistic features	• Table of contents, bulleted items, headers
		• Boldface font, font size, italics
	• Organization	• Sequential, description, cause and effect, compare and contrast, problem and solution
	• Visuals	• Maps, diagrams, photos, level of visual

Figure 4. Sample Text Complexity Chart

TOPIC/THEME ___ The Five Senses

I. TEXT/AUTHOR

| | GENRE | | NUMBER OF WORDS | EASE OF LANGUAGE | |
LITERATURE	NONFICTION INFO.	OTHER		Figurative	Word Choice
	X		P	N/A	P

The Five Senses: Tasting (Rissman, 2010)

PRESENTATION OF INFORMATION

Linguistic Features	Organization	Visuals
photos, glossary, index, headings, contents page	descriptive	1

COMMENTS: only one to two sentences per page, photos of ethnically diverse people, very basic book with only new vocabulary word possibly being umami
many labeled pictures—good introduction to feature
better for pre-K class

2. TEXT/AUTHOR

| | GENRE | | NUMBER OF WORDS | EASE OF LANGUAGE | |
LITERATURE	NONFICTION INFO.	OTHER		Figurative	Word Choice
	X		N*	N/A	P

Eyes and Ears (Simon, 2003)

PRESENTATION OF INFORMATION

Linguistic Features	Organization	Visuals
Diagrams	descriptive	1

COMMENTS: *like other Simon books—great for my own background knowledge far too difficult for my classes. But really great activities for my students great job of introducing technical vocabulary within context may use text to introduce hearing aid and color blindness may share a few sentences to show how author defines words in context

3. TEXT/AUTHOR

| | GENRE | | NUMBER OF WORDS | EASE OF LANGUAGE | |
LITERATURE	NONFICTION INFO.	OTHER		Figurative	Word Choice
	X		P	N/A	P

Our Senses: How Sight Works (Morgan, 2011)

PRESENTATION OF INFORMATION

Linguistic Features	Organization	Visuals
glossary, index, content, pg. headings, websites, DIVERSE fonts	descriptive	1

COMMENTS: little less basic than Rissman book, more vocabulary introduced pupil, iris, retina, colorblind), relates to students' lives-sunglasses reading warning signs, playing golf/tennis, discusses how animal eyes vary, text also would be great to illustrate use of diverse fonts

P = Positive   N = Negative

multiple pages will be needed to analyze texts pertaining to a specific topic. According to Ogle and Correa-Kovtun (2010), a text set should contain at least 8–10 titles on the content theme.

Along with listing the text and author, there is a place to mark an X for the genre of the text. Because teachers are expected to achieve a 50–50 balance between informational text and literature, it is important to note the genre. That way we can monitor the types of text we are using with students and ensure that we engage them with a wide variety of genres. We must remember that nonfiction includes both informational texts and other texts. (More details on informational text can be found in Chapter 2.) "Other" texts include hybrid texts or factual texts that do not contain linguistic features. Many texts for early learners are nonfiction, but they are not informational. Therefore, it is important to determine whether a nonfiction text is truly informational.

As the rest of the chart is completed, include the letter P (positive) or the letter N (negative) for each factor. For each item, determine if that factor is a positive and facilitates comprehension of the text or if it is a negative and hinders comprehension. If there is a large number of words in a text or if a text is extremely lengthy, then you know that word count may hinder a student's understanding of the text. We know that students can feel overwhelmed if they see a text with page after page full of words. Therefore, if the number of words in a text is excessive, then you would put an N under the Number of Words column, because the number of words is a negative and may hinder comprehension. After the chart is completed, the N can serve as a reminder that the number of words in the text may create an issue with students. Additional support may be needed to facilitate understanding of the text.

Under the Ease of Language column, determine if figurative language facilitates understanding of the text or hinders it. Young children may not understand some uses of figurative language, and figurative language can be confusing for English learners. Word Choice is an area where teachers need to pay attention to the types of words in the text. Are most of the words easy to understand within context? Do the words contain morphemes that can be taught? While the ELA CCSS want second-grade students to be able to recognize and read common prefixes and suffixes (RF.2.3d), third-grade students are expected to decode Latin suffixes

(RF.3.3b). More information for developing vocabulary will be shared in Chapter 5.

For the next area of the chart, Presentation of Information, you may decide to write words instead of a *P* or an *N*. Under Linguistic Features, it may help to identify italicized words, bullets, or other linguistic features that play a prevalent role in the text. Under Organization, I would consider writing *S* (sequence), *D* (description), *C-E* (cause-effect), *C-C* (compare-contrast), *P-S* (problem-solution). That way it is evident which type of organizational structure is used in the text and ensures that students are exposed to varied text structures. Finally, under Visuals, I would write a *1*, *2*, or *3* depending on the level of visual. White (2012) explains that there are three levels of visuals. The level of visual pertains to how data are categorized.

If the data in a graph are represented with one category, then the visual is a Level 1. If the data are classified under two categories, the visual is a Level 2, and if the information is classified under three categories, then we would label the visual a Level 3. The classification system shows that while visuals are important, they can vary greatly in complexity. A Level 3 graph would be more complex than a Level 1 graph.

Figure 5 shows three levels of visuals our young learners might be exposed to in informational texts. In the Level 1 graph, the students have to understand only the percentages of each way students get to school. The Level 2 graph requires that they look at how data are embedded in two categories. Students must examine both the groups of community workers as well as the number of third-grade students who interviewed each type of worker. Finally, in the Level 3 graph, students not only look at temperature but also at the months for two years. It is easy to see how the graphs become more complex for the reader to understand. Of course, visuals include more than graphs.

Maps are another type of visual that might have various levels. An outline of a state would be a Level 0 visual. However, an outline of a state that includes major cities would be a Level 1 visual. If the state also has dotted lines outlining the counties, then it is a Level 2. A Level 3 map would have data shown under an additional category. For example, a map of a large state such as Texas might have not only its major cities and counties marked, but also its different climates, identified with levels of shading. Along with listing the highest visual level contained in the text,

Figure 5. Three Levels of Visuals

Level 1

How Students Get to School

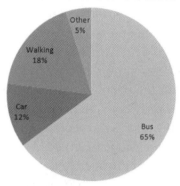

Level 2

Community Workers Interviewed by Third-Grade Students

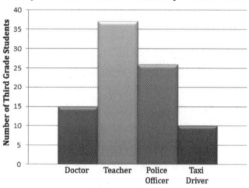

Level 3

High Temperature

it might be helpful to note the type of visual (e.g., graph, map) on the Text Complexity Chart.

The Comments section on the Text Complexity Chart is the perfect place to write down additional details that may need special attention. Perhaps the text contains unique names or dialect. Pronouns may also create issues. In fact, I recently received a text message from a middle school teacher because her seventh-grade students were struggling with figuring out pronouns when they read social studies texts. She said that the students saw *Rosa Parks*, *Mrs. Parks*, and *she* in the same chunk of text, which created confusion. If students in seventh grade are struggling with pronouns, we need to start focusing students' attention on pronouns at an earlier age. Think of the content knowledge these students have missed over the years because of the issue of pesky pronouns. As sophisticated readers, we can easily infer and understand text like that, but if older students are encountering difficulty, then clearly it is an issue of text complexity we need to address with our younger learners.

As Fisher and Frey (2013) point out, we must think about scope and sequence. What are we going to do to ensure that our early literacy learners are exposed to the different text complexity factors? If we continually focus our students' attention on font size and the use of headings and subheadings, chances are those factors will no longer create issues for students. However, the same students may not be prepared for text that contains other factors such as varying organizational structures or a large number of polysyllabic words containing morphemes. By completing the Text Complexity Chart, we have a better idea of the factors related to complexity that our students are being exposed to in the classroom. Therefore the chart can guide future text selection.

Perhaps our first graders are completing a "then and now" unit in social studies. We want to use quality informational texts that will capture our students' interests. After looking through various sources and talking to other teachers, we decide to use three texts written by Jennifer Boothroyd (2012): *From Typewriters to Text Messages: How Communication Has Changed*, *From Marbles to Video Games: How Toys Have Changed*, and *From Chalkboards to Computers: How Schools Have Changed*. After analyzing each text as shown in Chapter 2, we believe these texts contain up-to-date, accurate information. However, we still want to be sure to examine text complexity along with text quality.

Using the Text Complexity Chart, we note that each text contains a table of contents, page numbers, glossary, index, headings, and text boxes. Because some students are still developing an understanding of what an index is and none of them have seen text boxes, which draw attention to additional information the author wishes to share, these three texts might work well to further students' understanding of those linguistic features. We notice that none of the texts in the set contain subheadings or visuals beyond photos. We cannot have every type of organizational structure or linguistic feature represented in a text, and we would not want a text to. We, however, want to show our students how visuals with various levels of complexity can share information in a text.

Because the books were believed to be quality informational texts, there is no reason not to include them in the unit. We will probably want to supplement them with other print or digital texts related to the theme of "then and now" so that students can interact and engage with texts demonstrating a wider variety of complexity features. If we examine other materials and we still feel that certain aspects of text complexity are lacking, we can target those aspects in the next text set we use. The purpose of the Text Complexity Chart isn't to necessarily eliminate any texts from consideration. Rather, it is meant to monitor the various aspects of text complexity to which our K–3 students are exposed.

Keeping the Reader in Mind

As teachers, we are often concerned about English learners and those readers who struggle with text. We have to remember that the ELA CCSS do not tell us how to teach. They only provide the standards that must be met. The classroom teacher knows the students best. The key to helping students achieve with increasingly complex texts is to differentiate instruction with all children—we can't give them complex text and hope for the best. For example, English learners and struggling readers will need extra scaffolding. After determining what is causing them to struggle with a text, we can provide the support they need to improve their literacy skills.

At the lower grade levels, we can make a difference in how English learners and struggling early literacy learners will deal with text they encounter in future years. (A lot of the suggestions for teaching these students are actually good teaching practices for all students.) The ELA

CCSS do not expect that our K–1 students will be reading the complex text but rather that they will be introduced to the text through listening activities. That provides an opportunity to support students' language development, build background knowledge, and enhance their comprehension skills.

This brings up an interesting potential benefit to the ELA CCSS for those students who are struggling with reading. Prior to the CCSS, it was tempting to use high-interest, low-readability texts, or vocabulary-controlled texts, or even very limited text with those students possessing weak literacy skills. Meanwhile, our stronger readers were engaging with more sophisticated text, which was adding to their knowledge base. They were being exposed to a wider range of words, including technical words. They were engaging in sophisticated discussions that occurred naturally because of the quality and quantity of text. Our struggling readers, however, were not only continuing to have reading difficulties, but also experiencing a widening knowledge gap and were at a true disadvantage for future text expectations. Clearly, there are things that we can do with complex text to help struggling readers be successful (Ehri, Dreyer, Flugman, & Gross, 2007). Although it is helpful to have an assessment method to evaluate texts, we know that text complexity doesn't reside solely within the text. We as teachers must play a key role in making complex text accessible for all learners.

Helping Students Succeed With Complex Text

We have to assess and build background knowledge with all students. All children have had different experiences, and unless we determine what they know about the content it will be impossible to help them succeed with the complex texts. Many teachers I know find that virtual field trips work well with children. There are thousands of such trips available for free online, and many are appropriate for primary grades. A virtual field trip is a collection of interactive webpages related to a topic and grade level. These webpages are arranged in a format so that the class can progress through the links. Some visual field trips are even held in real time so that students can ask questions and talk to experts about the content.

There may be cultural content in a text that is not familiar to readers, such as a character's dialect or multimeaning words. As stated prior, idioms are difficult for most early learners, but they can be especially troublesome for English learners. We must view text through a culturally sensitive lens to determine what aspects of a text may be problematic.

We must also remember that literacy is a social act. Many of us have seen students engage much longer with a reading or writing task when they worked with others. Working with others allows children to learn from their peers. Providing time for students to reflect and share their viewpoints can help them achieve a deeper level of understanding when they read a piece of text (Nichols, 2006).

Many people in the educational field have been sharing the benefits of teaching with an inquiry approach with students (Almasi, 2008; Guthrie & Davis, 2003). In an inquiry approach, the students guide the instruction by searching for answers to questions that are important to them. According to Beach and Myers (2001), dialogue that arises through cooperative inquiry is one of the most effective ways for children to build a knowledge base. Haneda and Wells (2008) believe that this is especially true for English learners. Along with the benefit of constructing knowledge through an inquiry approach, students will develop collaboration skills that will be important for the rest of their lives. Few people work in isolation. To be successful in their careers, most scientists, teachers, mathematicians, and other professionals spend large quantities of time collaborating with others.

We all know the power of choice with children. Children, like adults, want to feel that their opinion matters and that they have a say in what occurs. Researchers and educators continue to emphasize providing choice in the classroom (e.g., Patall, Cooper, & Wynn, 2010; Reynolds & Symons, 2001). Let's consider offering a choice of how tasks are completed. Students can look at texts alone or with a peer. They can decide where in the classroom they want to look at texts. They might lie on the rug, sit in their seat, or curl up in a reading corner. When we are strengthening literacy and content area skills, the power of choice cannot be underestimated.

The Power of Reading Aloud With Our K–1 Literacy Learners

As discussed earlier in this chapter, the ELA CCSS state that our K–1 students are not expected to independently read complex texts during reading lessons. The texts they independently read will need to contain many decodable words and common sight words. It is only appropriate to incorporate more complex text reading with students in second grade and higher. However, that still means that we have to expose our youngest students to complex texts. Let's think about what can be done with our K–1 students first and then talk about how we can help our second- and third-grade students independently read complex text.

Reading aloud is important at all grade levels, and research supports sharing informational texts as part of our read-alouds (Smolkin & Donovan, 2001). Because we want to expose our kindergartners and first graders to more complex text than they can actually read independently, reading aloud is a great way to engage them with such texts. Many of us have been reading aloud to children for years, and the benefits have been well documented. When we read aloud to our students, we can make connections to other texts and to the world around them. It is also a great opportunity to not only build students' background knowledge but also to strengthen their academic language.

Research shows that for English learners, academic language takes much longer to develop than oral language (Hakuta, Butler, & Witt, 2000). This makes sense because oral language includes words that children use on a daily basis to converse with others in their surroundings. Academic language normally is not used in everyday conversations. Reading aloud informational texts will serve to introduce technical vocabulary and the various types of organizational structures found in content area text. This is especially important for English learners (Silva, Weinburgh, Smith, Barreto, & Gabel, 2008). As we point out to our students a cause-and-effect pattern in a social studies trade book on farmers or the steps listed in a science text on growing a pumpkin, we are exposing our students to various text structures and introducing words that they would encounter only in specific content areas. Ogle and Blachowicz (2001) emphasize the importance of students in the intermediate grades learning to identify text structure, but we can begin developing those skills at an even younger age. Activities such as this also allow students to use multiple texts. Students can discuss how the texts convey information, share the similarities and differences between the texts, and discuss which type of text they prefer. Research shows that young literacy learners can develop a deeper understanding of content through making intertextual connections (Heisey & Kucan, 2010).

By reading aloud we can also point out the unique linguistic features found in various texts and ask students why the author wrote the text.

Did the author want to inform, entertain, or persuade us? In addition, reading aloud is an opportunity to increase the background knowledge of our K–1 students in all content areas so they will be better prepared for independently reading complex texts. The power of reading aloud has been known for many years but, more recently, researchers have been focusing on the instructional value of reading aloud (Fisher, Flood, Lapp, & Frey, 2004). With the recent focus on these additional benefits, we now have an even greater reason to read aloud to our young students.

Making the Most of Read-Alouds

There are a couple of key points we will want to remember when reading aloud to our students. First, it is important to stop reading and discuss what has been read after short segments of text instead of waiting until the end of our reading to have a discussion (Sandora, Beck, & McKeown, 1999). This will allow us to orally engage our students in lively discussion at various points in a text. We can ensure that students understand the text, make connections to other texts or experiences students may have, and talk about aspects of the text that may have confused them. It may be helpful to preview the text and place sticky notes at appropriate stopping points. Those notes can also have discussion ideas or important points we want to share written on them. Of course, every text reading is unique because of the experience and background of the listeners. Therefore, the sticky notes are just points of reference, and as we facilitate the listening experience, we will more than likely find ourselves wanting to make other clarifications or noticing that some of our discussion suggestions are not necessary.

As I mentioned in Chapter 2, the use of generic nouns is a characteristic of informational texts. For example, a story about airplanes might have a sentence such as "The airline attendant helped the people find their seats on the plane," but an informational text about airplanes would state, "Airline attendants help people find their seats on planes." Research has shown that our youngest learners automatically notice characteristics such as generic nouns in informational text. In fact, kindergartners will gradually begin to approximate informational texts and reproduce it in their pretend readings (Duke & Kays, 1998; Pappas, 1993). If our K–1 students are approximating informational texts and reproducing it, then they are comfortable with the manner in which it is structured. This will help students to better understand informational text. This research provides an incentive to focus on informational text with our youngest readers. Through shared reading experiences, we can introduce our K–1 students to complex text and prepare them for future materials.

Engaging Our Second- and Third-Grade Students With Complex Text

Students in second grade and above are expected to independently read complex texts. We cannot be content with their understanding the texts through shared reading. Our challenge with these students is determining the best way we can help them to develop the skills to navigate such texts.

We know the importance of interest. Young children are naturally inquisitive about many topics, and we want to build on that curiosity. They want to know how plants grow, what makes things move, and information about almost anything else that they encounter. Therefore, personal interest in a topic is usually quite easy to develop with our early learners. However, when students don't have personal interest in a content area topic, we can build that interest. Situational interest is interest that occurs because of factors we can influence. It includes "task instructions or an engaging text" (Schraw, Flowerday, & Lehman, 2001). Although temporary, this situational interest can lead students to develop a personal interest in the topic and a desire to know more about it. It can also influence comprehension (Guthrie et al., 2006).

As discussed previously in this chapter, the power of choice is important for all learners. Think of how much more attractive a task is when we, as adults, are given choices. Children also like to make decisions about their learning. Perhaps we can select several texts on a topic and let students choose which one they want to read or in which order they want to read them. As stated earlier, students can also choose whether to sit in their seat, in a reading corner, or on the floor. Flowerday and Schraw's (2000) research suggests that providing choice for students who may not normally be interested in a task or text can increase interest. One suggestion they offer is that teachers can model how to make choices. Many of us already use think-alouds in our room. We can orally model for students our thought processes for making choices between texts or tasks.

Think about a topic you plan to teach your students in the near future. If possible, think about a content area topic that students in past years have found less than exciting. Then determine how you might be able to engage your current students with the topic and develop situational interest through choices that may be provided. Is there a way to provide choice related to texts? Is there a way the task can be completed in ways that still require children to engage with the text? Try out your ideas the next time you teach the topic and then reflect on what occurs. Did you gain any valuable insight related to choice that might be used to guide future content area instruction?

Similar to choice, variables related to the organization of text are also key in creating interest. Even though we assess the elements texts contain that make them complex, we cannot forget to evaluate the quality of a text. Texts that are well organized, vivid, and relevant to students have been shown to create a higher level of situational interest (Harp & Mayer, 1997; Wade, Buxton, & Kelly, 1999). More information on selecting texts is provided in Chapter 2.

Important Strategies for Working Complex Text

When students encounter challenging texts, they must be able to apply reading strategies to help them comprehend the material. While having a shared reading experience with K–1 students, we have ample opportunities to make our thinking explicit. We can model the following strategies to help students understand complex text:

- Rereading text
- Asking ourselves questions about a text and answering them
- Monitoring comprehension
- Visualizing
- Making inferences
- Analyzing text structure

Many of us already use these strategies with our young learners in shared text situations. However, the key is to get the second- and third-grade students to internalize these strategies and be able to implement them on their own. We must scaffold students so that they can use these strategies independently. Scaffolding can be done through a gradual release of responsibility model (Pearson & Gallagher, 1983).

The gradual release of responsibility model begins with the teacher having all of the responsibility for successfully completing a task and eventually moves to a situation where the students have all of the responsibility (Duke & Pearson, 2002). This movement occurs through scaffolding. According to Routman (2003), when there is a gradual release of responsibility, the teacher begins by demonstrating how a task or strategy is performed. Then the students have guided practice. After that, the teacher encourages the students to take more responsibility. As young learners begin practicing and then applying the strategies, the teacher serves more as a coach to encourage, validate, and clarify as necessary. The gradual release of responsibility model has been shown to be a successful model for teaching writing, developing comprehension, and working with English learners (e.g., Fisher & Frey, 2003; Kong & Pearson, 2003; Lloyd, 2004). The stages are not black and white, and students may go back and forth between the levels of assistance they need as they attempt different texts and tasks. However, through informal observation and evaluation, the teacher can help determine if students are internalizing strategies and whether they need more assistance in the process.

TRY IT OUT

Research shows that good readers monitor their reading, whereas struggling readers are often unaware when they lose meaning while reading a text and are less likely to reread (Johnston, 2004; Otero, 2002). Using the gradual release of responsibility model, model the rereading strategy to a small group of students. After a week or so, evaluate whether students internalized the strategy and are able to use it independently. If they are not able to do so, reassess how you might provide further scaffolding for those students who struggle so that they can use the strategy successfully with future texts.

Activities for Strengthening Students' Competence With Complex Text

The purpose of the following activities is to provide opportunities for students to engage with increasingly complex text. Through a variety of activities that they complete individually, with a peer, or as a class, K–3 students can become comfortable with informational text and develop a better understanding of pronouns, visuals, and figurative language. The goal is to engage students in fun activities that reinforce their literacy learning while they make connections to the content areas.

Going on a Text Hunt

Everyone loves a good scavenger hunt, and when students are hunting for linguistic features they are developing an important skill at the same time. This collaborative activity introduces students to the linguistic features they may encounter in informational text and attempts to make the terms for those linguistic features a part of their speaking vocabulary.

How It Works

1. Before starting this activity, assess what the students know about informational text features. There are many features that might be found in texts, but the number of linguistic features focused on in this activity will depend on the age of the children. Kindergartners and first graders may focus only on five key features so that they learn them well, while second and third graders may have prior knowledge of certain features and can easily develop an understanding of more features found in informational text. Possible features to focus on include font, bold words, table of contents, headings, subheadings, photographs and captions, graphs, labeled diagrams, maps, bullets, glossary, and index.

2. Explain to students that they are going to be learning about an important type of text, informational text. Show them an informational text and a narrative story. See if they can compare and contrast the texts. Explain that there are informational texts written on many interesting topics. Show a few texts that might appeal to the students. (There aren't too many students who wouldn't be interested in either *Monster Trucks on the Move* [Nelson, 2010] or *Spiders* [Bishop, 2007]).

3. Let students staple sheets of paper together to form a book. This book is going to serve as a guide for their scavenger hunt. (It might be a good idea to add extra sheets for features students learn about later in the year or features they want to include in their guide that aren't taught.) The students are going to create a guide on informational text features. The title for the guide might be Informational Text Features.

4. One by one, talk about each text feature on which you want to focus. As you talk about a text feature, write its name on the document camera or interactive whiteboard, and show the students two or three examples of that feature in printed texts. These texts can include books, newspapers, and magazines written on specific topics such as airplanes or cars. Talk about the purpose for the linguistic feature and why it is an important element in an informational text.

5. After students write the name of the text feature at the top of a sheet in their guide, have them look through magazines and newspapers to find an example of it. They can cut out the example and glue it on the appropriate page. (Drawing the features is another option.)

6. Repeat steps 4 and 5 for each feature you want the students to learn in the activity. *If time is limited, this is a good stopping point in the activity. The rest of the activity can be completed on another day.

7. Once the student guides are created, it is time for the scavenger hunt to begin. Divide the class into small groups. Give each group of students an assortment of books to examine. Perhaps mix in some narrative texts that have none of the linguistic features. Give each group of students a labeled sticky note or bookmark to mark where each of the linguistic features is located.

8. Direct students to go on a text hunt and find an example of each linguistic feature in the informational books. If there are multiple books with examples of one type of feature, some children may be able to find what they believe is the "best" example.

9. Afterward, allow the small groups to share their findings with the rest of the class.

PRC2

Partner or buddy reading has been used in classrooms for years. PRC2, or Partner Reading and Content, Too, is different because it was designed by Ogle and Correa-Kovtun (2010) to support English learners with content area text. However, everyone can gain from the activity. With this strategy, students have an opportunity to create questions, answer questions, use technical terms, and develop knowledge of content vocabulary and concepts.

How It Works

1. Assign each student a partner who is reading at a similar level and has similar interests. Then give each pair a content area text on a topic studied.

2. Have the students skim through the entire text looking at headings, pictures, and other features to get a general idea of the contents.

3. Instruct partners to read the pages on each two-page spread silently.

4. Instruct both partners to reread their page and think of a question they might ask about the page.

5. Then one person from each pair reads a page or assigned section aloud and asks a question of the listening partner. After answering the question, the partners talk about the page. That discussion provides both students with an opportunity to develop a deeper understanding of the material and an opportunity to orally use the vocabulary and concepts.

6. Step 5 is repeated so that students have an opportunity to switch roles. The reader becomes the listener and vice versa. The students continue to read the rest of the material in this manner.

Additional Suggestions

Students who have limited experience with partner reading or creating questions are going to need extra scaffolding with this activity. Therefore, it may be necessary to demonstrate the activity in a fishbowl-type setting so that other students can watch as the activity is modeled with a student.

Do You See What I See?

We all have heard that a picture paints a thousand words, but that is true only if we understand the picture. Students can have difficulty when confronted with a graph or map. If that occurs, no words are painted and no information is gained. White (2012) believes there are 34 features that can either make text easier or more difficult to understand. One of those features is visuals. White feels that the level of data embedded in a picture (e.g., graph, map) can create confusion for students. This activity draws students' attention to the importance of visuals.

How It Works

1. Begin by letting students look for graphs in newspapers, magazines, and digital texts. These graphs might include pictographs, pie graphs, or bar graphs. After finding examples, students can glue their findings on a large sheet of paper or re-create in a drawing those they may find in a digital text.

2. Discuss the reason authors use graphs in their texts. Do students notice anything about the graphs? Why do the graphs have a title? How is a pie graph different from a bar graph? What shape are the graphs? How do students think pie graphs and bar graphs got their names?

3. The students can also learn about how one child, Nan, made a bar graph with her class in the text *Let's Make a Bar Graph* (Nelson, 2013). This short text is geared for the youngest of children because each page contains a photo and only one or two sentences. The text also contains features such as a glossary and an index, which are often seen in informational text.

4. After talking about the book, brainstorm types of charts students might create about their classroom.

5. As a class, create a graph or two on large sheets of chart paper. Talk about the type of information shown in the graphs.

6. Take one of the graphs and put another piece of chart paper next to it. Ask the students what type of information is shown in the chart. Write that information in sentence form on the second sheet. Point out the difference between the two pieces of chart paper. Isn't it amazing how many words it takes to give the reader the same information found in a graph? Discuss the phrase, *A picture paints a thousand words*.

7. After the students have an understanding of how to create a graph, tell them that they can use the computer to create graphs! The Create A Graph interactive found at www.nces.ed.gov/nceskids/graphing/ gives students an opportunity to create five types of graphs: bar, line, area, xy, and pie.

Students can also select the font, background, and grid color; location of legend; and whether it will be a 2-D, 3-D, or shadow graph. If students are new to graphing, they can create simple graphs by clicking on Create a Graph Classic. After the product is created, a graph size can be selected and the graph can be printed.

8. Let students look through informational texts to see if the authors use any graphs. Have students mark the graphs with a sticky note. Then discuss their findings.

9. Summarize the lesson by reviewing why graphs are used in text. Talk about how good readers are always looking for visuals.

Additional Suggestions

This activity is designed to be an introduction to visuals. With older students, or students who have more sophisticated literacy skills, consider modifying the activity by introducing a bar graph that is a Level 3 visual or maps containing various levels of data. (See Figure 5 in this chapter.)

This activity can also be a good follow-up activity for Psst! Did You Know?, an activity discussed in Chapter 6. If that activity is completed, the class can refer back to the text it wrote. Students can use the pages created in their book to come up with ideas for how they could create visuals to add to the information. What type of information might students want to include about lunch? Would they like to create a graph showing their favorite lunches? What about the page on students? Would they like to create a graph showing how many students are boys and girls or how many students are 5 or 6 years old in the class? Talk with students about how they might best show the information. A graph with only the age of the students or the gender of the students might be more easily displayed in a pie graph rather than in a bar graph.

The Pesky Pronoun Patrol

Pronouns can be pesky for all students. Although pronouns can help students understand content when the pronouns clearly refer back to nouns, unclear pronoun references or text with a many pronouns may cause confusion. Further, pronouns with the clearest references back to nouns can be confusing for struggling readers. By serving on the Pesky

Pronoun Patrol, K–3 students can develop a better understanding of this text complexity issue.

How It Works

1. Tell the students that they have been invited to join the Pesky Pronoun Patrol! Sometimes authors use words to replace names in a text, and those words hide the real identity of the person. Students' job is to hunt down those pronouns and make them tell the name of the person they are replacing or hiding. To get their official membership card as a member of the Pesky Pronoun Patrol, students must be able to figure out those tricky pronouns. Put a chunk of text up on an interactive whiteboard or on a large sheet of chart paper. With young students, this may be as short as four to six sentences. A chunk of social studies text that focuses on a famous person works well because there will be many pronouns in a short piece of text.

2. Read the title and the rest of the text, emphasizing reading from top to bottom and left to right. After reading through the text, ask the students to chorally read the text. Discuss the text and read it one more time. By now, even young students will have most of the text memorized.

3. Go back and read the title and first sentence of text. Who is the text about? Tell students they must now search for other words that are hiding the name of the person in the text. With the youngest students, this may take a lot of scaffolding. Read the second sentence and ask if any words refer back to the person. If necessary, emphasize the pronoun and ask questions until a student gives the appropriate word.

4. As pronouns are found, write them on a sheet of paper hanging in the classroom titled "Pronouns Captured." Take a card or small piece of paper with the name of the person written on it, and have a student tape the card or paper so it covers up the pronoun in the text. Continue reading through the text searching for other pronouns. As you find the words, add them to the Pronouns Captured sheet and cover up the pronoun.

5. At the end of the activity, chorally read the list of pronouns captured. Then reread the text with the name of the person in place of each pronoun. Ask the students if the text makes sense. Some students may agree that it makes sense but that it sounds funny. Use this opportunity to explain that pronouns can be good. Students' job on the Pesky Pronoun

Patrol was only to learn about pronouns so that pronouns can't play tricks and confuse them. When students read a text, it may sound boring or repetitive to constantly read someone's name. Perhaps students should let the pronouns loose and uncover them on the text. Remove the cards, and have the class read the text one more time. Students might also get a badge showing that they have figured out the pronouns' tricks and that they are now official members of the Pesky Pronoun Patrol.

I Am Thinking of a Book

As we introduce informational text to our youngest students, we have to be sure that they clearly understand how informational text varies from narrative text. This is a quick game that can be used to show how the two types of text vary and to reinforce the differences between the texts. As discussed previously, researchers have shown that even kindergartners are capable of noticing those differences (Duke & Kays, 1998; Pappas, 1993).

How It Works

1. Prior to starting this activity, create sentence strips using sentences from books the students have been listening to recently. One text should be narrative and one should be informational, and the two should be related to some extent. For example, both *National Geographic Readers: Frogs!* (Carney, 2009) and "Frog and Toad Are Friends" from the *Frog and Toad Collection* (Lobel, 2004) involve frogs but are different types of text. Be sure to obtain two copies of both texts used.

2. Tell the students that they are going to play a game. Here are sentences from two of their favorite books, but in which book do the sentences belong? Can they help? Talk about how the two texts differed.

3. Show them the two texts and review the titles.

4. Read one sentence strip and ask students to tap their head with an index finger as soon as their brain figures out which book contains the sentence. Students shouldn't shout out the answer but tap their head as a way to show they have the answer.

5. When many students are tapping their head, tell them to show thumbs up when they hear the name of the text that contains the sentence. If using

the frog texts, statements such as "Frog and Toad went sledding" might be easy, but can the students tell you *why* they know that sentence didn't come from the informational text? Perhaps they will mention that real frogs can't go sledding or that Frog and Toad are names.

6. After sorting the sentence strips into two stacks (one for each text), divide each into two more stacks. Then divide the class into four groups. Give each of two groups a stack of sentence strips for the narrative book and give each of the remaining two groups a stack of sentence strips relating to the informational text. Each group will also get a copy of the text where the sentences are believed to originate.

7. Ask the students to determine if their sentences are in the text.

8. When students are finished with the task, bring the entire class together to discuss the activity. Discuss how the writing in narrative and informational texts varies. For example, in narrative texts, there are often animals that have been given human characteristics. For informational texts, generic nouns are usually used and facts are included. You can end the activity by orally rereading the texts with the students or drawing their attention to other differences in the texts such as photographs and illustrations.

Additional Suggestions

You can make this activity more challenging by using a variety of texts. Some narrative and informational texts written on the same topic are not as easy to differentiate. For example, the award-winning text *A Frog in a Bog* (Wilson, 2007) is a narrative text, but it doesn't contain frogs that eat ice cream or a character named Frog. However, even young students will begin to pick up on the fact that sentences such as "He flicks one tick…" is from a narrative text because of the "he" reference.

Say It Again

Adults constantly use figurative language when they speak. It doesn't take long to realize that using such phrases is like speaking a foreign language to children. I find my own son questioning why I want to "run" to the store, and he gets excited every time I say something is "icing on the cake." Young children think literally, and we as adults use a lot of figurative phrases in day-to-day living. For English learners, these phrases can be especially confusing.

Shanahan and Shanahan (2008) found that figurative language is especially common in social studies texts. Older students often encounter terms such as *guerilla war, great divide, cold war, coat of arms, baby boom, iron curtain, civil war,* and more. Therefore it is important to help students at the earliest of ages to understand that what is written or said can often mean something entirely different from what the speaker or author means. Our goal isn't to have young students memorize such phrases but instead to have them be on the lookout for them. Whenever figurative language is encountered in content area text, it is important to discuss it so that it doesn't interfere with comprehension.

How It Works

1. Begin by using figurative language in a natural manner while talking with your students. Perhaps you note how well behaved they are and let them know they make you "happy as a clam." Or someone may complete an activity easily, and you can mention that the activity was clearly a "piece of cake." It won't take long for students to ask what you mean.

2. Tell students that sometimes words mean something other than what they think they mean. Ask the students if they have ever heard the phrase, "Let's hit the road" when their families wanted to go somewhere. If so, let someone explain the meaning. If not, then let the students guess what they think the sentence means. Does it really mean physically hitting the road?

3. Share and discuss a book that contains examples of figurative language. Then put several of the texts in the classroom library so students can continue to enjoy them. Figurative language is difficult to learn. The more experiences students have with figurative language, the easier it will be for them to understand it. Although Fred Gwynne's (1976) *A Chocolate Moose for Dinner* is still popular with primary teachers, there are more texts that can be shared. In fact, in recent years there have been so many quality texts published that it should be easy and quick to locate them. Denise Brennan-Nelson (2003, 2004, 2007, 2009) has written many books that play on words and share idioms: *My Momma Likes to Say, My Teacher Likes to Say, My Grandma Likes to Say,* and *My Daddy Likes to Say* are four of her books that explain a variety of adages. Within the

pages of her rhyming and rhythmic picture books, students can not only read common idioms that they may have heard adults say, but they can see the historical background and trivia for each idiom. Older students may find the historical part especially interesting and search out meanings for other figurative language on the Internet. Other personal favorites include Marvin Terban's (1983) *In a Pickle and Other Funny Idioms*, Loreen Leedy and Pat Street's (2003) *There's a Frog in My Throat! 440 Animal Sayings a Little Bird Told Me*, Will Moses's (2008) *Raining Cats and Dogs: A Collection of Irresistible Idioms and Illustrations to Tickle the Funny Bones of Young People*, and Catherine Snodgrass's (2004) *Super Silly Sayings That Are Over Your Head: A Children's Illustrated Book of Idioms.*

4. Next, list figurative phrases that you think the students may have heard or may encounter on an interactive whiteboard or document camera. Figure 6 is a list of example figurative phrases that may be shared, but there are many more that can be found easily on the Internet or in books.

Figure 6. Examples of Figurative Language Phrases

A bird in the hand is worth two in the bush	Hit the hay
A drop in the bucket	Hit the road
As pleased as punch	Horsing around
Birds of a feather flock together	In one ear and out the other
Black and white	Lighten up
Busy as a bee	Mad as a wet hen
Butterflies in the stomach	Over your head
Cold feet	Penny pincher
Cold shoulder	Piece of cake
Crawled to a stop	Raining cats and dogs
Early bird gets the worm	Spill the beans
Face the music	Trip you up
Feeling blue	Win hands down
Foot loose and fancy free	You are what you eat
Happy as a clam	

5. Select one of the figurative phrases. Tell students that they are going to play charades. You want them to act out the literal meaning of the phrase. After students act out a phrase, see if anyone can tell you what it means. If someone knows the meaning of the phrase, see if he or she can use it in a sentence. If none of the students recognize the phrase, use it in a familiar context—for example, "Anna was about to take an important test, so she had butterflies in her stomach." Talk about why people may use that figurative phrase. What would it feel like to have butterflies in the stomach? What does their stomach feel like when they are really nervous?

6. After reviewing the figurative language, have each student fold a sheet of paper in half. Then have students draw a picture of both the literal meaning and figurative meaning of one of the phrases on each half of the paper.

7. When everyone is finished, invite each student to read his or her phrase. Let the other students see if they can remember the meaning. Then let the student show the pictures he or she drew. The pictures can then be combined to create a text for the classroom, or students may donate the book to an English learner classroom because second-language learners often struggle with figurative language.

8. Encourage students to try out the phrases whenever they can during the day. Students might ask another teacher or principal if it is raining cats and dogs outside. Perhaps students will go home and try out one of the phrases on their parents and let the rest of the class know the next day how the phrase was used and what their parents' reaction was.

A Look Inside One Classroom

A first-grade teacher chose to introduce the idea of figurative language to her students during a unit on the sun and moon. The teacher began by asking her students what they thought was meant when they heard "Once in a blue moon" or "Everything under the sun." The students talked about how they thought it meant that the moon turns blue and that the sun is over everything. Each of the students drew a picture of the literal meaning on a sheet of paper.

Then the class chorally read an informational big book, *Finding the Moon* published by Delta Education (2003). The text has one sentence per page, so the students could chorally read through it. The students talked about the text and the visuals. Within the pages of this text, readers

Figure 7. First-Grade Student's Literal and Figurative Drawings of Two Figurative Language Phrases

Note. The top drawing shows "Everything Under the Sun" and the bottom drawing shows "Once in a Blue Moon."

learn the phases of the moon, why it shines, and its characteristics. The book ends with a page stating that the sun shines on the moon. Many students did not understand that final page. The teacher had a classroom set of a short informational text about the moon, and she had the class read it. After the students read and discussed the second text, the teacher explained that there is an idiom about the sun and the moon. *Idiom* was a new term for the students. The teacher explained that the phrase "Everything under the sun" means *everything*: If you talk about everything under the sun, then you talk about *everything*. You talk for a very long time.

Then she explained the phrase "Once in a blue moon" and said that if students rarely do something, then they can say they do it once in a blue moon. The teacher and the students talked about how figurative language is a different way of expressing thoughts. The phrases had different meanings than the individual terms *sun* and *moon* in their science unit. The students were then asked to draw a picture to represent the figurative meaning. Figure 7 shows one first-grade student's drawings of both literal and figurative interpretations for both examples of figurative language.

Although figurative language can be confusing for students, it is important that they learn to recognize it. Learning idioms helps students to understand phrases of speech they hear older students and adults use. It also helps for students to understand idioms so that they can comprehend content area material. By introducing idioms in an engaging manner with our K–3 students, we are helping them begin to understand figurative language and also preparing them for the types of phrases they will encounter in the upper grade levels.

REFLECTING BACK AS WE MOVE FORWARD

We are expected to use complex content area texts with students as they develop their content area knowledge. While our K–1 students can be introduced to these texts through shared reading experiences, our students in second grade and above must be able to independently read the texts. To effectively facilitate student learning with complex texts, we must rethink how we engage our students in shared reading experiences, how we develop their interest in content area information, and the way we develop effective reading strategies. Through a gradual release of responsibility model, we can help students to develop the strategies they need to be successful with informational text in social studies, science, and other content areas. By reexamining how we use complex text in the classroom, we can strengthen our students' literacy skills and enable them to develop an even deeper knowledge of content information.

CHAPTER 5

Important Words Are Not Always Big and Bold: Developing Vocabulary Skills

Vocabulary is important. We can't make powerful connections between the content areas and reading and writing without a strong vocabulary. Often when people talk, they don't have to use precise words because the listener can determine what is being said through other cues (Nagy & Scott, 2000). However, when we are thinking about the printed word, those cues aren't available. It is necessary use precise words when writing. Students have to be aware of the importance of specificity when selecting words for writing. For students to write to learn across the content areas, they will need an adequate vocabulary (Jones & Thomas, 2006).

TRY IT OUT

Show students the following written sentence: *The animal is big.* You cannot determine the size of the animal by simply reading the sentence. Now, say those words to students. Emphasize the word *big* with expression and drag out its pronunciation. At the same time, you might hold your arm out at about shoulder level with the palm down to make them think that you are showing the height of the animal. After orally reading the sentence, ask students what the size of the animal is. Many of them will believe the animal is huge. When a student writes a word such as *big* in text, it doesn't carry the same meaning as when it is spoken because the context of the word is gone. This is just one way to demonstrate for K–3 students the importance of using precise vocabulary when writing. To write with precise vocabulary, students have to learn the vocabulary terms first and really *know* the words so that they can use them correctly.

Many of us grew up taking weekly vocabulary quizzes. Each week we had a list of isolated words to study. These words might have been the highlighted words in a textbook chapter or the terms listed at the front of each textbook chapter. We spent copious amounts of time trying to memorize the words, and hopefully we passed the vocabulary quiz at the end of the week. However, did we really remember many of the words for very long or were they just temporarily stored in our short-term memory long enough for us to pass the quiz? Did that type of activity help us to build word consciousness or an interest in words? Were we able to develop the depth of knowledge we needed to apply the words to new situations? Vocabulary knowledge has always played an important role in content area learning at the elementary grades, but the way those in the education field view vocabulary is changing. As students encounter increasingly complex text and as we raise our literacy expectations with the ELA CCSS, students are going to need to learn even more challenging terms. At the same time, we are realizing the complexity of vocabulary knowledge. In order to make powerful connections to the content areas, we must redefine what it means to know a word.

Vocabulary plays a key role throughout the ELA CCSS too. In fact, the Vocabulary Acquisition and Use section of the Language strand contains a list of standards that students are expected to meet beginning at the kindergarten level. Vocabulary includes "general academic and domain-specific words and phrases" (L.3.6). Our young literacy learners are expected to understand figurative language, multimeaning words, compound words, and meaningful word parts. They are also expected to be able to distinguish between shades of meaning among similar words. This is no easy task. Vocabulary expectations are found in other strands of the ELA CCSS as well, referring to comprehending text, decoding Latin suffixes (RF.3.3b), and reading with accurate expression (RF.1.4; RF.2.4; RF.3.4). All of these expectations require students to have well-developed vocabulary skills.

As we seek to develop vocabulary knowledge in our young students, we must keep in mind that both depth and breadth are important. As K–3 teachers, we must not only consider which content area vocabulary terms must be taught, but also ensure that students really know the terms. Although being able to explain a term is important, our young students must learn to apply terms to new contexts and use their understanding of terms to extend their knowledge base. Vocabulary knowledge is critical for reading and meeting the ELA CCSS, and it has been shown to be a symbol of a well-educated person (Beck, McKeown, & Kucan, 2002). To help our K–3 students truly know words, vocabulary instruction must take place throughout the school day and across all content areas.

Helping Our K–3 Students to Really *Know* Words

In Chapter 1, we discussed Shanahan and Shanahan's (2008) three-tier model explaining how literacy knowledge develops. Our early literacy learners are learning high-frequency words at the basic literacy level and then building an even larger knowledge base of words, including those not normally found in their oral language, at the intermediate literacy level. Then at the disciplinary literacy level our students are taught vocabulary terms, or technical terms, they might encounter only in specific content areas.

It is easy to see the relationship between their model and Vacca and Vacca's (2008) three types of vocabulary that children encounter. Vacca and Vacca believe that there are general terms, which coincide with Shanahan and Shanahan's basic literacy level. Then there are general, or multimeaning, words that might have a general meaning in everyday language but that take on a new meaning in math, science, or social studies. The highest level of words consists of specialized and technical terms or, as I hear many teachers refer to them, Tier 3 terms. Although high-frequency words were discussed in Chapter 3 along with other foundational skills, general and specialized vocabulary terms are also important so that our K–3 learners can make the content area connections. Research has shown that vocabulary is a significant factor in comprehension (Fisher, Frey, & Lapp, 2008; McKeown & Beck, 2006) and in overall school achievement (Beck et al., 2002). As teachers, we must identify the academic vocabulary and phrases in texts that students must understand and support our students' learning of those words.

The problem is that students encounter a lot of vocabulary words in the content areas. Our job is to determine the best way to teach the terms. Research suggests that there are many ways we can help young students know words. One suggestion is to teach students to use glossaries and dictionaries. In fact, according to the ELA CCSS, students in second grade are expected to be able to use both glossaries and dictionaries (L.2.4e). Blachowicz, Fisher, Ogle, and Watts-Taffe (2006) encourage us to focus on developing word consciousness and to help students develop word learning strategies. Finally, we can focus on helping students understand how vocabulary concepts relate to one another.

Word Consciousness

When we develop word consciousness, we are attempting to build an awareness of and an interest in words (Graves & Watts-Taffe, 2002). If we can get our young literacy learners excited about learning new words, they will pay more attention to words and want to learn more words. Interest can be a strong motivator in the way students approach unknown words. We might encourage students to share interesting words they hear or see, create word pictures, and even play games with the words. A K–3 classroom can have puzzles, joke books, games, word flashcards, picture dictionaries, local text, and other literacy materials that encourage students to engage with new words. These types of activities might work especially well for multimeaning words and figurative language. Both types of vocabulary can be difficult for young children.

TRY IT OUT

What types of activities do you incorporate into your classroom each year to develop word consciousness or to get students interested in words? Regardless of their grade level, students need to develop an awareness of and an interest in words. Look online and in print journals and talk to other teachers. Think about content area topics that introduce many unfamiliar words to students. Then find two or three creative activities you can try this year with your students to help them realize how much fun it can be to learn new words.

Word Learning Strategies

When we think of explicitly teaching words, I am sure many of us think that the idea is practically hopeless. There are so many new words that students will encounter in the content areas. One way we can target specific words is through the use of student-created picture dictionaries. We are not only helping our K–3 students learn to use dictionaries and glossaries, but also reinforcing their knowledge of new words by having them draw a picture and write the definition.

Another way we can develop vocabulary is through teaching Greek and Latin roots (Blachowicz & Fisher, 2000). When roots are taught, students are learning not only specific words, but also roots and affixes that can be used to decode other words they may encounter in the content areas. Although this may be seen by some in the educational field as a strategy for older students, Biemiller (2005) believes that by the time students are in second grade they should be able to use roots as a vocabulary word. This belief is reflected in the ELA CCSS at the second-grade level, where students are expected to use root words to determine unknown words (L.2.4c). In fact, students as young as kindergarten age are expected to be able to start using common inflections and affixes to read unknown words (L.K.4b). Table 4 contains a list of roots and affixes suggested for primary-grade students (Padak, Newton, Rasinski, & Newton, 2008).

Word Relationships

In order for students to develop a deep knowledge of words, they must understand how the words relate to other words. This is true for all early literacy learners. In the Language section of the ELA CCSS, kindergarten students are expected to explore the relationships among words (L.K.5). At first grade and above, students are expected to be able to categorize words, identify relationships between words and their use or real-life connections, and understand subtle differences in words (L.1.5; L.2.5; L.3.5). Through a discussion of content area terms and how they relate to one another, students can develop a more thorough understanding of the terms.

Talking With Students

Risley (2003) believes that the best way to increase vocabulary for students is through talking with them. Although he is referring to the importance of parents and caregivers engaging their children in conversation, there is no reason to believe that the power of talk is any less valuable in the classroom. As many of us are aware, children who grow up in low-SES

Table 4. Roots and Affixes for Primary/Elementary Students

Type	Sample	Meaning
Prefixes	• *co-, con-* • *de-* • *ex-* • *in-* • *pre-* • *re-* • *sub-* • *un-*	• with, together • own, off of • out • not (*"negative"*) • before • back, again • under, below • not (*"negative"*)
Bases	• *audi-, audit-* • *graph-, gram-* • *mov-, mot-, mobil-* • *port-* • *vid-, vis-*	• hear, listen • write, draw • move • carry • see
Numerical bases	• *bi-* • *tri-*	• two • three
Suffixes	• *able, -ible* • *-er* • *-est* • *-ful* • *-less*	• can, able to be done • more • most • full of • without

Note. From Getting to the Root of Word Study: Teaching Latin and Greek Root Words in Elementary and Middle Grades by N. Padak, E. Newton, T. Rasinski, and R.M. Newton, in *What Research Has to Say About Vocabulary Instruction* (p. 13), by A.E. Farstrup and S.J. Samuels (Eds.), 2008, Newark, DE: International Reading Association. Copyright 2008 by the International Reading Association. Reprinted with permission.

homes may experience greater difficulty developing adequate vocabulary because many of them will begin school with a more limited vocabulary than their peers (Coyne, Simmons, & Kame'enui, 2004). Therefore, we must focus on strengthening students' vocabulary as early as possible in formal schooling and also pay attention to the needs of individual students who may require more extensive help with vocabulary skills. Vocabulary plays such an important role in comprehending content area material that we must ensure all students get the reinforcement needed. We don't want our struggling readers to fall further behind as content area material becomes more complex.

Because social language develops much more quickly for English learners than academic language, which can take five to nine years (Hakuta et al., 2000), we must also find ways to provide additional reinforcement and support for our English learners to develop their vocabulary knowledge. We know that learning vocabulary terms in English is vital for English learners (Folse, 2004). English learners must have regular opportunities to talk and use their vocabulary in order to internalize the information (Shanahan & Beck, 2006). If our English learners can't *say* a word in English, it will be extremely difficult, if not impossible, for them to *read* the word. We also know that figurative language and multimeaning words can be confusing for early learners, but this type of language will require explicit instruction with EL students.

Finally, as discussed in previous chapters, students can benefit greatly by working collaboratively to build their literacy knowledge. This is especially true with second-language learning. Group work can play an important role in developing vocabulary knowledge (Baker, Gersten, Haager, and Dingle, 2006; Peregoy & Boyle, 2001). One idea that works well with our youngest learners is to have emergent literacy learners work together to sort pictures of content area concepts into categories (Bear, Helman, Templeton, Invernizzi, & Johnston, 2007). Furthermore, research supports the power of reading aloud. It is an extremely valuable activity not only for students whose native language is English but also for those who are learning English (Biemiller, 2004; Calderón et al., 2005). Through orally sharing a text in class, asking questions, and discussing the material, all students can strengthen their vocabulary.

Let's look at how that might look in a K–3 classroom. For example, if a first-grade class is studying needs and wants and goods and services in social studies, the teacher may read aloud informational texts such as *What Do We Buy? A Look at Goods and Services* (Nelson, 2010) and *What Can You Do With Money? Earning, Spending, and Saving* (Larson, 2010). The contents of the texts can tie easily to students' lives outside of class and as questions are asked and answers are given, the teacher can confirm that students understand terms such as *producer, consumer, income, saving, spending, earning,* and *donate.* The class might even create a chart that shows a list of goods used and services provided for the school. Individually, students may create a list with one column titled "Needs" and one titled "Wants." After sharing with a small group, students may determine that some items in the Needs list should be moved to the Wants column. As a follow-up activity, the teacher can cut and paste pictures of goods and services and needs and wants that students might experience on individual concept cards. Then students can work to sort the cards into groups. English learners may not know all of the words associated with the pictures. If necessary, they can ask a peer for assistance. Also, as the teacher looks over the cards and discusses the concepts with students, it will be clear which terms are still not in the English learners' vocabulary and may require further reinforcement.

Activities for Expanding Students' Vocabulary Knowledge

All of the following activities can be used effectively with our K–3 students. With our youngest children, some of the activities may need to be completed collaboratively instead of independently, but the activities will still be valuable. The activities build prior knowledge, reinforce roots and affixes, encourage the consideration of word relationships, introduce figurative language, and reinforce the learning of content-specific terms.

ABC+ Brainstorming

Many teachers already use ABC Brainstorming with students. With ABC Brainstorming, students try to think of a word beginning with each letter of the alphabet that ties to a topic. This activity extends that idea. ABC+ Brainstorming is a fun, versatile vocabulary activity that requires minimal preparation time on the part of the teacher. This strategy not only helps kids think about their prior knowledge before a thematic unit or topic begins, but also allows them to build upon that knowledge through discussions with the rest of the class.

How It Works

1. Prior to starting a content area topic, explain to students that they are going to brainstorm words that relate to the topic. (Broad science and social studies terms such as *desert*, *motion*, *celebrations*, and *plants* work best with this activity.)

2. Give each student a copy of the ABC+ Brainstorming Sheet on page 165 in the Appendix. Explain to students that you want them to write a word related to the topic that begins with each letter of the alphabet. The sheet can be completed as a whole-class activity on the smartboard, or

older students can complete it individually. Students don't have to think of a word for *every* letter, but they should think of as many as possible. For example, students might not be able to think of a word that begins with *A* or *B* for *desert*, but perhaps someone thinks of *cactus* for *C*. *Cactus* is then written next to the letter *C* under the column titled "Brainstorm." (Even if students will work independently on this activity, the class will probably want to brainstorm the first few letters together the first time the activity is used.)

3. After students have written as many words as possible in the Brainstorming column, they can work with a peer to think of additional words they might list under the column titled "Other Ideas." Students are expected to understand the words they are writing on the sheet, so this activity requires the students to have a discussion before any terms are written. Be sure to emphasize word specificity: Students should think of words that tie to the content area and aren't general words that can be used with any topic. Nobody should be writing the word *the* for the letter *T* or the word *an* for the letter *A*.

4. Then bring the class back together and discuss the words the students thought of during their brainstorming. If there are any blanks left on the ABC+ Brainstorming Sheet, students can choose one of the words discussed in class and add it to their list.

Additional Suggestions

This activity can be modified easily. If students have completed this activity once or twice, it might be fun to use this as a prestrategy and poststrategy. Allow the students to brainstorm on the ABC+ Brainstorming Sheet prior to starting a content area unit. Then collect the sheets. At the end of the unit, give the students back their sheets. See how many more content-specific terms they can come up with on their post sheet. Students will love to see how their vocabulary has grown.

Build-a-Word

Have you thought about how many words are created through common affixes and roots? Many young students are familiar with the phrase "reducing, reusing, and recycling." Look at all of the affixes and roots that make up that phrase. Although we want to explicitly teach specific content area terms, think about how many additional words students can figure out by knowing frequently used prefixes, roots, and suffixes.

Many technical terms found in the content areas are created through combining Latin and Greek roots. In fact, some educators and researchers believe that nearly 75% of English words are based on Latin or Greek roots (Padak et al., 2008). Rasinski, Padak, Newton, and Newton (2007) gathered the Latin and Greek roots shown in Table 4, and those roots and affixes are ones K–3 teachers might consider teaching. As other roots and affixes are encountered in content area material, the morphemes can be included in this activity. It isn't possible to include *every* morpheme that students encounter, so it is essential to use morphemes they see most frequently in their content area texts. The ELA CCSS Language strand recognizes the power of building words and requires that our young learners be able to use commonly occurring inflections and affixes such as *–ed, -s, re-, un-, pre-, -ful, -less* (L.K.4b; L.1.4b) and root words (L.2.4c; L.3.4c) to figure out unknown words. Build-a-Word encourages students to create new words using Latin and Greek roots as well as other frequently seen affixes and root words.

How It Works

1. Select several quality informational texts on a topic. Show students the books but cover the title. Tell students that they are going to become word builders. They must put on their hard hats so that they are ready to construct or build words. First students will have to figure out the titles of the texts. Write the affixes and roots for each text title on a card. All of the affixes for a text should be on the same color card.

2. Then divide the class into groups. There should be one group for each text you selected for the activity. Give each group a color-coded set of cards. Ask students if they can determine the name of the text. Use this opportunity to explain that some roots and affixes don't make sense together so students know those can't be combined to form a word. With the youngest students, struggling readers, or even those students who haven't manipulated word parts before, it may help to capitalize the first letter of each word in the title in order for the students to complete the activity. In addition, students can do a picture walk through the text first to get clues for figuring out the title. However, if the students need a

challenge, you can just as easily eliminate clues such as capitalized letters and picture walks.

For example, the following affixes can be combined to create a title for a text that might be used with a Then and Now unit in social studies: *to, board, -s, compute, chalk, -s, how, school, -ed, have, change, -s, from, -er*. When the affixes and roots are combined, the text title becomes *From Chalkboards to Computers: How Schools Have Changed* (Boothroyd, 2012).

3. The next step is to select the affixes or roots you want to focus on in the text, which will depend on the book selected. The aforementioned informational text comprises many compound words including *lunchroom, classroom, backpack, chalkboard, filmstrip, sometimes, handwriting, keyboard, textbook,* and *schoolroom*. Therefore, with a text such as this one, teachers may choose to use the text to reinforce students' understanding of compound words. In this instance, tell the students that they will put two words together to make a new word. These new words are called compound words.

4. After finding all the compound words in the text, write each root word in the compound words on a card. For example, the word *classroom* would be written as two word parts. One card would have *class* written on it, and another card would have *room* written on it. Repeat for each compound word in the text. Give each student a card. Ask the students to find another student who has a root word that can be added to their root word to build a compound word that can be found in the text. Then have each student work collaboratively with his or her partner to write the compound word on a piece of paper and draw a picture of what they think the term means.

5. Once all the students have finished drawing their pictures, ask the students to share their creations and discuss each of the words. Have they ever heard of the word? Does the word make sense? Were they able to figure out the compound word's meaning based on its two parts?

6. Chorally read the compound words one more time. Afterward, point out that sometimes the suffixes *–s* or *–ing* are added to words, including compound words. Talk about how those suffixes can build a word.

7. Now it is time to read and discuss the content area text. As the text is read aloud, ask students to listen for the compound word they created. The word builders can snap their fingers two times or touch their ears when they hear their compound word.

8. After the text is read, be sure to put it in the class library so that students can go back and read it later. Also, extend the activity to reinforce the concept targeted. If compound words were the focus, then start a chart titled "Compound Words" and ask students to bring in any compound words they may hear or see at home to add to the chart. Also, take the remaining texts on the topic and create root cards for any compound words in those texts, making sure to put the roots for each text on a different color paper. Place each set of root words in a word builder envelope. Students can work in small groups as time allows to create other words related to the topic.

Add It Up

In the early elementary grades, students should be introduced to multimeaning words. These terms might include homophones, words that sound alike but are spelled differently, and homonyms, words that sound alike and are spelled alike but have different meanings. Both types of words include math terms, so it is important that students understand that words can have more than one spelling and meaning. Many teachers choose to introduce the topic of homophones and homonyms with narrative texts. Books such as Fred Gwynne's (1976, 1988) *A Chocolate Moose for Dinner* and *The King Who Rained* are popular with teachers. Students and teachers also enjoy Marvin Terban's (2007) *Eight Ate: A Feast of Homonym Riddles*, Brian P. Cleary's (2007) *How Much Can a Bare Bear Bear? What Are Homonyms and Homophones?*, Gene Barretta's (2010) *Dear Deer: A Book of Homophones*, and Nancy Loewen's (2007) *If You Were a Homonym or a Homophone*. After students have been introduced to the concept of homophones and homonyms, it is time for them to Add It Up!

How It Works

1. Figure 8 contains a list of examples of homophones and homonyms. You can also find many more examples online. Decide which homophones and homonyms your students are ready to learn. You might want to divide and conquer and teach some of the more familiar words on the list at the beginning of the year and save some of the more difficult words for later.

Figure 8. Examples of Homophones and Homonyms

act	change	ground	miss	right*	strike
ant*	check	hair*	moose	ring	son*
ate*	color	hand	nail	rock	swallow
back	cut	high*	note	roll*	tie
band	deer*	jam	one*	run	tip
bar	duck	land	park	seal	top
bark	dry	lap	part	see*	trip
bill	eye*	leaves	pass	sink	two*(3)
block	face	left	pen	slip	volume
box	fair*	letter	pick	space	watch
break*	fall	lie (3)	plane*	spring	wait*
by*(3)	fine	mail*	play	stamp	wave
can	flu*	mass	pupil*	star	wood*
cent*(3)	fly	mine	rain*	state	yard

Note. * denotes a homophone; (3) denotes that there are three meanings of the word.

The words with an asterisk in Figure 8 are homophones. If there is a 3 next to a word, it means that there are three meanings for the word.

2. Divide the class into small groups of students. Write one of the words from Figure 8 on the board. Students in the first group must collaborate to come up with the multiple meanings of the word. They might choose to act out a meaning for the word, draw a picture of one of the meanings, or use the term in a sentence explaining it. The group receives 2 points for each multimeaning word it gets correct. If a group doesn't know the meanings for its term, the next group gets to try to define the term. If certain terms are unfamiliar to many of the students, consider using the term again the next time the game is played.

Modifying the Activity

To challenge students, you might pick an equal number of words that are not homophones or homonyms. Mix those words in with the ones you want to review. If a word is written on the board that is neither a homophone nor a homonym, and the group of students whose turn it is agrees that it has only one meaning, the group receives 2 points. If the group thinks there is another spelling for the term or another meaning and the group is incorrect, it does not receive any points.

We're Related

As part of the target skill Vocabulary Acquisition and Use, students are expected to be able to explore word relationships. Although kindergartners and first graders are expected to be able to sort common objects into groups (L.K.5a; L.1.5a), kindergartners through third-grade students are expected to identify real-life connections between words and their use (L.K.5c; L.1.5c; L.2.5a; L.3.5b). To successfully explore word relationships, students need to have a deep understanding of the terms.

I have created two sets of steps for completing this activity. To determine which set of steps to follow, first select the target skill. Is the goal to work on merely sorting words or focusing on their real-life connections?

How It Works (For K–1 Teachers Focusing on Sorting Skills)

1. Introduce the idea of categories with *Sort It Out!* by Barbara Mariconda (2008) or a similar text. Within the story, the reader is introduced to a pack rat who saves everything. As pages are turned, the reader is encouraged to guess what several items in a pile have in common. The items might be the same color, have the same texture, come from a tree, be the same shape, be made of the same material, or have some other similarity. Talk about the fact that many of the objects in the text are related in some manner.

2. On a medium-sized box, write "We're Related." Inside the box, place approximately 25 small objects.

3. Explain to the students that you have a problem for them to solve. There are many items inside the box, but they are all mixed up. You need the students' help to see if there is a way some of the objects might be related. Perhaps some objects are the same color. Maybe some of the objects are found in the home kitchen. Other objects may be found outside in nature.

4. Have the students sit in a circle on the floor. Open the box and display the items in the middle of the circle. As you pull each object out of the box, ask a student to identify the object and tell what he or she knows about it. This discussion will help build the students' depth of knowledge about the objects and enrich their vocabulary.

5. Then give the students a short period of time to think about similarities among some of the objects. If students struggle, you might initially make a suggestion such as "Do you see several objects that might be used to build something (e.g., nail, piece of wood, sandpaper)?"

6. When students name items in a group, group the objects off to the side. After a category is identified, ask if others in the class agree. This is also a good time to help students refine their categories. If the class is studying nutrition in health, students may select an empty carrot bag, a granola bar box, a small milk carton, a chocolate bar wrapper, a cookie recipe, an empty egg carton, a photo of a cake, and an orange peel and say they are all related to things we eat. When students form large groups of items, ask them if they can find a way to form two smaller groups of objects from within that larger group. This makes students refine their thinking. In this instance, the students might decide that instead of one large group related to foods they eat, they can have a group of healthful foods and another group of foods that are not healthful.

How It Works (For K–3 Teachers Focusing on Words and Real-Life Connections)

1. Create word cards with phrases showing real-life connections between words and their use. Figure 9 contains examples of possible connections that students might describe. You will want to add to the list as you think of other real-life connections between words and their use.

2. Write each phrase from Figure 9 on a sentence strip. Underline the word and the real-life use. For example, on a strip that reads "Describe places

---

Figure 9. Real-Life Connections With Words and Their Use

Items that are personal
Places at home that are cozy
Foods that are sweet or sour
Clothing that can be scratchy or itchy
Things that can be frightening
Places outside that can be beautiful
Toys that can be entertaining or fun
Activities that can be tiring
Adults who are helpful or friendly
Places in school that are colorful
Events that can be loud or noisy
Holidays that can be filled with traditions
Months that can be busy
Animals that can be frightening
Things that can be humorous or funny

outside that can be beautiful," underline the words *places outside* and *beautiful*. Roll up the sentence strips and tie a piece of yarn around each one. Put the rolled-up phrases in a box with the label "We're Related."

3. With older students, the class may be divided into groups, but for kindergartners and even first graders it may be better to use this as a whole-class activity. Explain that one student will pull a sentence strip from the box, and the students have to explain how the underlined words can be related.

4. Have one student in the class come to the front and pull a sentence strip out of the box. Read the phrase to the class.

5. Tell the students you want them to think about the task. (Describe <u>places outside</u> that can be <u>beautiful</u>.) The students need to think of beautiful places they have been to outside. Ask younger students to draw a picture as an answer. Second- and third-grade students can either draw pictures in their groups or create a list for the answer.

6. Have students share the ideas they came up with in a whole-class discussion.

Words That Pop

Beginning in kindergarten, children should begin to distinguish between shades of meaning with similar terms. While kindergartners and first graders are expected to distinguish among similar verbs (L.K.5d; L.1.5d), second- and third-grade students are expected to be able to distinguish between adjectives and words in general (L.2.5b; L.3.5c). Distinguishing among similar terms will not only broaden students' vocabulary, but also help them to be better writers. I use the term *kernel* to refer to a word that students often use excessively in their speaking and writing. My goal is to take those kernel words and get the students to create Words That Pop.

How It Works

1. Depending on the age of the students, select a kernel word on which to focus. Although we don't want students to stop using kernel words entirely, we also don't want to see the words overused. Again, with kindergartners or first-grade students, it may be best to start with verbs because the definitions can be shown easily through actions. (Some kernel verbs to consider using are *say, walk, look, throw, believe,* and *eat.* Some kernel adjectives are *scared, thin, small, large,* and *pretty.*)

2. Take the kernel word and write it in the middle of a piece of chart paper. Then talk about how it is a kernel word. You want to take the kernel and create more specific words that can pop right off the paper, just like popcorn. Words That Pop are words that are more vivid. They paint a picture in the reader's mind.

3. Ask the students if they have any ideas for a word that can replace the kernel word. Then ask them if they have suggestions for ways they may be able to come up with Words That Pop. Perhaps they can look online or in printed dictionaries or ask adults or older students in other classrooms for suggestions. Students may even decide to ask people in the community. Tell students that the goal is to come up with Words That Pop. As they come up with suggestions, the new words will be added to the chart. Later in the week, the class will complete a special activity with the words.

4. As the students bring in Words That Pop, discuss the words with the class. Then use the word in a sentence to see if the new word can replace the kernel word. If the class agrees that the word can replace the kernel word, add it to the chart. If the word is a verb, have students act out each word before it is added to the chart. This physical movement will help the students to remember the word. Students can also act out the words that have already been added to the chart. Have a class discussion on how the most recently added word is similar to or different from other Words That Pop on the chart. Figure 10 is an example of what charts may look like with the kernel words *walk* and *say* and possible Words That Pop that might replace the kernel words.

5. After about a week, the chart is going to be complete. At that time, copy the words on individual cards. As you hold up the word cards, say the word aloud. Students can repeat the word and act out the term if it is a verb. If the students are older, they may be working on adjectives and other words. If so, they can just read the word.

6. See if students can get into a line showing a continuum of Words That Pop. If the kernel word was *talk*, students might line up from the quietest word to the loudest word that replaces *talk*. If the kernel word is *walk*, they might try to line up from the slowest way to walk to the fastest way to walk. There is not one correct answer because who can say whether *yell* or *scream* is louder, but you know that the students holding cards with *yell* or *scream* written on them should be somewhere near the opposite end of

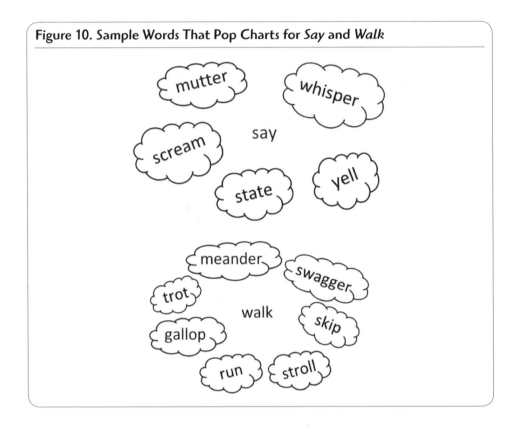

Figure 10. Sample Words That Pop Charts for *Say* and *Walk*

mutter

whisper

say

scream

state

yell

meander

swagger

trot

walk

skip

gallop

run

stroll

the line from a student holding a card with the word *whisper* written on it. Then allow students who are not holding cards to take turns reading a word card and using the word in a creative sentence.

7. Leave the charts visible in the room so that students will get to see and hopefully use the Words That Pop again. Also, older students can use the charts as a way to make their writing come alive. After the students write a text, they can seek out some of the kernel words that they have been discussing in class and see if their writing might be better if some of the kernel words were replaced with Words That Pop.

Creating a Word Shape

This strategy can serve as a great motivational tool for K–3 students. At the end of a thematic unit or after the students know a number of vocabulary terms related to a concept, they can use the computer to create a visual incorporating the terms. This strategy can be tied easily to other vocabulary strategies discussed in this chapter and used as a culminating activity for a unit.

How It Works

1. As a final review activity, ask the students to work in pairs to brainstorm vocabulary terms related to the topic. Encourage them to think about the quality of terms instead of the quantity of terms. Explain to students that they must be able to explain the terms that they brainstorm. If they don't know the meaning or are having difficulty with the spelling of the word, they can look in a picture dictionary or another source to determine the meaning before they use the word.

2. Then have the students go to Tagxedo website at www.tagxedo.com/app.html.

3. Students click on the Load button. Then they type the words in the box next to where it says Enter Text. Then they click on Submit.

4. Students then click on the arrow button next to Shape and select the shape that best connects to the topic. There are more than 30 shapes available. Here are some possibilities:

Shape	Topic
piece of fruit	healthy eating habits
bus	vehicles and transportation
cloud	weather words
Lincoln's head	basic government terms

Students can even select to use a word as a shape. For example, if students are studying outer space, they might choose the word *moon* after typing in the words they brainstormed pertaining to outer space.

5. Students can print their word shape to share with friends and family. Creating a word shape can also serve to motivate students to display the words they used in a brief written text on a topic.

A Look Inside One Classroom

A second-grade teacher used the Tagxedo website in combination with other activities related to a unit on continents. Leading up to the creation of the word shapes, she shared with her students several informational texts. Along with a printed informational text and a digital text, the class also skimmed the *Atlas of South America* (Foster, 2008). After sharing the texts, students looked at a map of South America. Then as students talked about what they had learned about South America (see the PWIM activity in Chapter 3), the teacher wrote phrases and vocabulary terms on a map. Afterward, the class created a collaborative text summarizing what they knew about South America. The teacher wrote this text on the document camera, providing yet another opportunity for the second-grade students to see their words in print. Figure 11 shows the class text.

Students created word shapes after the class text was written. The teacher demonstrated on a computer how to create word shapes containing vocabulary terms on the Tagxedo website. Then the students were allowed to work individually to create their own word shapes. By analyzing the word shapes created, the teacher is able to see the terms the students are using as well as note difficulties students may have with some of the words. Some students chose to use the outline of South America for their shape, while others chose to use a heart shape. By being allowed to choose the shape, students felt they had a choice within the activity. A wide range of students enjoyed this class activity. In Figure 12A and 12B, we see two examples created by second-grade students.

The word shape in Figure 12A was created by Danielle, a student who qualified for gifted and talented instruction and demonstrates quite advanced literacy skills. When you look at her word shape, it is clear that

---

Figure 11. Class Text About South America

South America

Out of the seven continents South America is the fourth largest. There are mountains, a desert, and a rain forest. The Andes Mountains have a cold climate. Llamas and alpacas live in the mountains. The desert is on the west coast. There are snakes and cacti. In the rain forest there are two kinds of animals: the jaguar and pumas. One of the biggest birds in the world lives there. The Andean Condor lives near the Andes Mountains. Some of the people in South America speak Portuguese. Some people live in rural areas. There aren't any schools or doctors. Sao Paulo is the largest city. Brazil is the largest country. South America would be a cool place to visit.

Figure 12. Examples of Second-Grade Students' Tagxedo Word Shapes About South America

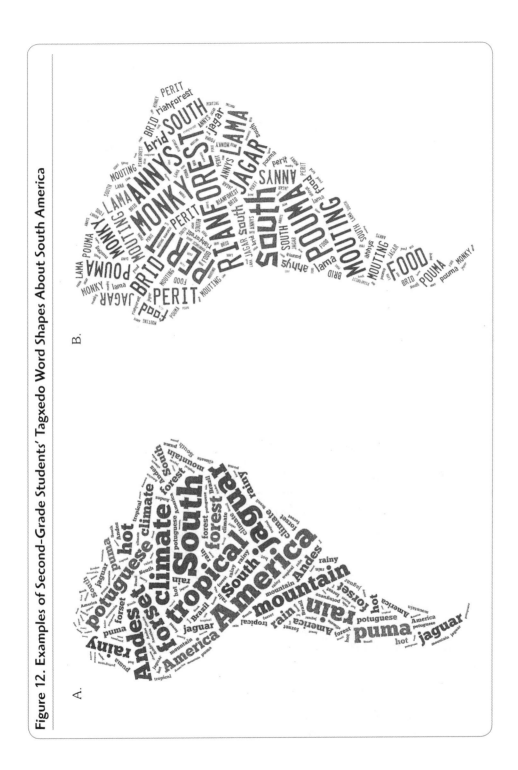

A.

B.

she focused on the climate and geography of the region. The word shape in Figure 12B, which is equally impressive, was created by Luisa, who is an English learner. Luisa chose to focus on the different types of wildlife found in South America in her word shape. The words *perit* (parrot), *monky* (monkeys), *jagar* (jaguar), and *pouma* (puma) show that she is attempting to spell academic vocabulary phonetically. Even though Luisa is not as advanced with her academic literacy skills as Danielle, she did an excellent job with the activity.

After the word shapes are completed, the teacher may analyze the vocabulary terms the students used to expand upon their interests. Finding additional texts about the animals found in South America or on other continents can help reinforce Luisa's background knowledge and spelling as she learns more about the topic. In addition, because Danielle shows an interest in the geography and climate, it might be feasible for her to work with other students or an adult to create a map of South America using symbols to show that information. Creating a word shape is a great way to reinforce vocabulary with young literacy learners and to make connections to the content areas, but the activity can also provide information that can lead to teachable moments with a wide range of students.

Vocabulary Visits

This strategy, which was originally developed by Blachowicz and Obrochta (2005), focuses on vocabulary terms in any content area. Students build their content knowledge through listening to quality informational texts read aloud and by thinking about relationships among concepts. This activity has a preassessment and postassessment component that can help students and teachers see how much students are learning.

How It Works

1. Select at least five informational texts that tie to a content area topic. You will want to locate chart paper, markers, and sticky notes for the activity.

2. Review the informational texts and determine key vocabulary terms that you want to use when discussing the texts.

3. Create a Vocabulary Visit poster with some pictures, photos, or illustrations that will engage the students in a discussion of the topic.

4. Introduce the topic to the students and help them to share prior knowledge.

5. Give students a Vocabulary Visit: Before the Visit Sheet (see page 166 in the Appendix), and ask the students to draw an illustration and list any terms they think of when they hear the topic. Save this sheet so that it can be used as a preassessment of their vocabulary knowledge on the topic.

6. Share the poster with the class, and ask students what they see. As students contribute words, write them on a sticky note and add to the poster. Be sure to serve as a facilitator. When student give a word, you can mention how it ties in to other concepts, ask students questions about the term, have them act out a word, or encourage them to extend answers.

7. Place sticky notes on the poster in a manner that shows word relationships.

8. Read the first informational text aloud to the students. Use the Thumbs Up procedure to involve the students: Students show a thumbs up if they hear one of the words on the poster.

9. After the reading, discuss what the students learned and, if necessary, add a few terms to the chart.

10. The students can then write a brief note about a fact that they thought was particularly interesting or share something that still confuses them.

11. Place the text in the classroom library, so students can look at it later. The words on the chart can also be put on small cards. Students can use them for word sorts or categorize based on semantics.

12. Keep the Vocabulary Visit poster prominently displayed in the classroom, and repeat the activity with each informational book.

13. At the end of the entire Vocabulary Visit, have the students complete two writing activities. One writing activity will be time intensive. Students might create an informational brochure on the topic to show their families what they learned or a picture dictionary containing some of the terms that they can use as a review guide. Students need an authentic audience, format, and purpose for the writing. Ask students to complete the Vocabulary Visit: After the Visit postassessment sheet on page 167 in the Appendix. On it, students will list all the words they can now write on the topic.

14. Compare the Before the Visit and After the Visit sheets. Of course, it isn't enough for students to only list the words. Informally assess whether

the students used the terms in the longer writing activity they completed and in the oral classroom discussions. The more the words are used, the better the chance that students will remember them.

Talking Drawings

This strategy, which is one of my favorites, was originally developed by McConnell (1993). It not only strengthens content area vocabulary, but also draws on the benefits of reading aloud to students. It also provides the students with an opportunity to incorporate visuals in their work. Although this strategy can be used across the content areas, it is especially beneficial for science. Because science texts contain a great deal of visuals, this activity serves as a way to reinforce their importance in gaining meaning from text.

How It Works

1. Decide which science topic you will teach and select a quality informational text that you wish to share with the students. (Chapter 2 provides guidelines for selecting informational text.) Read through the text several times before sharing it aloud. Many teachers find it difficult to orally share informational text because of a lack of experience using informational texts in a read-aloud and because the text's linguistic features disrupt the flow when they are reading. Use a sticky note or other method to mark several places where you might want to pause and discuss the text's contents with students.

2. Introduce the science topic. Explain to students that before you share a book on the topic you want them to individually draw an illustration about the topic. This is an excellent time to talk about the importance of visuals in text and the information they can provide to readers. Where have students seen visuals? What did students learn from the visuals?

3. Allow the students to draw a picture on the topic. Tell them that the picture should show what they know on the topic. They can label items or phrases or just draw.

4. After students finish drawing, have them share the drawings with the class.

5. Read and discuss the selected text aloud to students.

6. Ask students to modify their drawings or, if it is easier for them, they may choose to create an entirely new drawing on the topic based on the text you shared. Encourage students to label parts of their illustrations and use any new technical terms they heard in the text.

7. Talk about the strategy. Have students share their illustrations with the class. Ask students to identify what they changed on their illustration after they listened to the text or to share both drawings if they chose to create a new one. Students will also strengthen their vocabulary by listening to other students explain their drawings. Some students will mention terms others did not notice. This is a great time to encourage students to go back into the text to explain why they added certain information.

A Look Inside One Classroom

A first-grade teacher decided to tie this strategy into a science unit she was teaching on plants. She began by asking her students to draw whatever they knew about plants. She told students they could label or write words as part of the activity. Figure 13A contains the initial picture drawn by Tyisha. In the picture, she drew a rainbow, a tree, the sun, and plants. She chose to draw and label rabbits and the roots on the flowers. After the activity, the teacher read and discussed *From Seed to Plant* (Gibbons, 1993) with the class. Then students had the opportunity to draw another picture showing what they learned about the topic. Figure 13B shows Tyisha's second drawing, which was completed after listening to the text. The drawing indicates that she has learned a great deal about the topic: It looks much more scientific than her first drawing. Instead of just drawing a tree, Tyisha labels the tree and seeds. This is similar to the way Gibbons provides diagrams with labels. Then Tyisha asked her teacher to write other words. As she dictated the words, the teacher wrote them on the paper. When any of the students questioned if specific terms were used to label certain parts, the teacher directed the students to look back into the text. For example, Tyisha asked the teacher if one thing she drew was called a *pod*, and the teacher had Tyisha confirm she was correct by looking back into the text before the teacher wrote the word.

Talking Drawings is a great way to connect informational texts with content area learning, and it is an easy way to show students how much they can learn about a topic through reading and discussing informational text. It also works well with a variety of ability levels because students are

Figure 13. A First-Grade Student's "Talking Drawing" About Plants

A.

B.

Note. These drawings were made before and after the teacher read a book about plants to students.

only comparing their own drawings. Everyone can show growth through this activity.

REFLECTING BACK AS WE MOVE FORWARD

Within this chapter, we discussed the importance of helping students to thoroughly *know* vocabulary terms. Our young learners must develop breadth of terms as well as depth of terms. Students need not only to learn the vocabulary, but also to remember the terms. To help them do this, we must develop word consciousness, and we must actively involve our students in vocabulary learning. K–3 students also need repeated opportunities to use the terms. This isn't going to be possible with weekly vocabulary tests or even by asking students to look up definitions. We need to get students orally sharing, reading, and writing a variety of content terms, and we do this by using a wide variety of strategies to build word knowledge (Lehr, Osborn, & Hiebert, 2004). We must immerse our students in content area words.

CHAPTER 6

Creating Writers Who Are Content Area Communicators

The focus on writing has slowly been changing. Many of us still have emotional scars from the dreaded "What I did last summer" essay that was a hallmark of going back to school. Another common writing practice from the past was to ask students to write on a daily prompt or sentence starter or to write a narrative. These activities, though done with the best of intentions, are, thankfully, on their way out (albeit slowly). Although we thought we were helping students get over writer's block, the activities probably help to explain why our requests were often greeted with cries of "But I can't think of anything to say!" Beginning in kindergarten, the Writing strand of the ELA CCSS focuses on using writing to communicate information, which gives K–3 students a purpose for writing. To meet that purpose, students will need to consider the format, audience, and topic. This may appear to be a demanding task, but research with young children supports having even our earliest learners create informational texts (e.g., Read, 2005).

A number of educators and researchers have expressed concern about the writing quality of our students. In fact, in 2002, the majority of 4th-, 8th-, and 12th-grade students on the National Assessment of Educational Progress did not master their grade-level writing expectations (Persky, Daane, & Jin, 2003). Further, the College Board warned that we must place a heavier emphasis on writing (National Commission on Writing, 2003). To prepare our students for the writing tasks demanded in later grades and in real-life contexts, we are going to need to rethink our writing focus with the youngest of literacy learners.

Although the ELA CCSS Writing Standard requires students to write narrative texts (W.K.3; W.1.3; W.2.3; W.3.3) throughout the grade levels, the majority of the standards focus on writing that supports content area learning. According to Knipper and Duggan (2006), "Writing to learn is an opportunity for students to recall, clarify, and question what they know about a subject..." (p. 462). By engaging our K–3 students in this type of writing, we can help create content area communicators. *These* writing activities not only result in stronger writing skills and deeper content knowledge, but also incorporate the type of writing that students will do long after they leave our classrooms (Fisher & Frey, 2004). We all know it isn't enough to require extensive writing in our K–3 classrooms. If we consider only the amount of time students spend writing, I don't think we will be happy with the results even if we require that our students write frequently. Although having extensive opportunities to write is a good start, students need to have knowledgeable teachers who facilitate and offer guidance as they try to communicate their thoughts. Writing is another example in life in which we realize that practice alone doesn't necessarily make perfect. Although teachers may be hesitant to intervene too much with students' writing, students need explicit instruction so that they can convey information, opinions, and thoughts. We must provide intervention and support and then gradually withdraw our scaffolding so that students can become competent independent writers (Corden, 2007). To create young content area communicators, we need to provide appropriate instruction.

Keys to Good Writing Instruction

One essential thing to remember as we work with these young learners is that we want them to develop positive dispositions toward writing. If students decide at a very young age that they don't like writing, it will be more and more difficult for them to become content area communicators. Luckily, young children come to school with a curiosity about the world that is unparalleled. They can't wait to learn! We are entrusted with that energy and enthusiasm, and we must think carefully about how we will foster their writing growth.

Confidence, Persistence, Passion

According to a review of the qualitative literature on writing conducted by Piazza and Siebert (2008), confidence, persistence, and passion are three key elements that may account for a writer's disposition. We have to keep those three areas in mind from the moment we begin working with our young students. We want them to have confidence in their ability to be successful with communicating their thoughts. We also need students to remain engaged with the process and persist with their writing because writing well takes time. Finally, writing requires passion. If students are interested in writing and want to write, they will be more successful in doing so. By keeping in mind what we want students to develop at the earliest of ages, we can put them on the path to being successful writers in the later grades. As K–3 teachers, we play a significant role in young literacy learners' attempts to write. If they fail to develop confidence, cannot remain engaged with the writing task, or dislike writing, it can have a ripple effect through the remaining years of schooling and beyond.

Authenticity

Most important, we want to engage students by providing authentic writing activities. That means we want the writing activities inside our classrooms to replicate the type of writing activities that occur in students' lives outside of the classroom (Duke, Purcell-Gates, Hall, & Tower, 2006). Our writing activities should require students to create authentic texts for authentic purposes and authentic audiences. Perhaps there is a class pet that students take home on the weekend. Creating a list of pet care guidelines for the student's parents entails writing that has both an authentic purpose and format. If students create a content area display, they can also create signs to help other students understand the display. Students may also enjoy creating an invitation for the school principal to watch a play they have been practicing. It is amazing what students can do when they write for a real audience. Research by Wollman-Bonilla (2001) shows that even first-grade students can demonstrate an awareness of audience when they have an authentic and responsive audience and are asked to write for real purposes. Our early literacy learners are ready for the challenge of writing to learn.

Think about the content area topics you teach each year. Then work with other teachers to brainstorm a list of 10 authentic writing activities that students might enjoy and that tie to those content areas. These activities should have an authentic format, audience, and purpose. Writing thank-you notes to the adults who helped with the school carnival might work for older students, while a whole-class thank-you note for the head volunteer of the festival might work for the younger students. If a local veterinarian visits students, they might create a thank-you gift for their guest. The students as a class can discuss their favorite parts of the veterinarian's visit and research more information about a veterinarian's work in informational texts and digital sources. Then students can create an illustrated informational text about veterinarians that can be displayed in the waiting room of the veterinarian's office for other children to read. Try several of the ideas that you've brainstormed and meet again to discuss the results.

When we think about the writing we do outside of class, most of it is tied to informational writing. Therefore, we need to help students learn to create informational/explanatory texts. Hansen (2001) found that using quality informational texts helps students get ideas for their own writing. Likewise, research by Calo (2011) has shown that nonfiction texts can serve as a connection between writing and reading with students in first and second grade and help connect literacy skills and the content areas. We want to provide our K–3 learners with opportunities to examine various texts and write based on information they learn (Stahl & Shanahan, 2004).

But Our Students Are Still Learning How to Write

As K–3 teachers, we might find the ELA CCSS writing expectations to be especially overwhelming. Our students are so young and often have very little writing experience prior to schooling. However, preschoolers and young children who do not attend preschool often have an opportunity to express themselves prior to formal schooling through a variety of activities including drawing. In fact, it is common for children to combine many symbol systems such as dramatic play, drawing, and writing (Siegel, 2006). Although not all children come to school writing their letters or even recognizing their letters, they more than likely have picked up a pencil, crayon, or piece of chalk and have drawn something. This experience with drawing can be a starting point for writing. The Writing strand of the ELA CCSS allows us to reach children where they are and build upon the knowledge and experiences they bring into the classroom.

The Writing strand encourages drawing beginning with the youngest literacy learners and requires that kindergartners use drawing, dictating, and writing to compose texts (W.K.1; W.K.2; W.K.3). Therefore, we can build upon what our youngest literacy learners already know as we guide them in their writing to learn. This makes educational sense because drawing is similar to writing. When children construct a drawing, they must take into consideration audience, purpose, and form (Tompkins, 2009). Ogle, Klemp, and McBride (2007) believe that children need to be taught to blend visual and narrative content, and the ELA CCSS reflect that belief. Even the youngest children who are just learning to write can begin the process of writing to learn.

Of course, drawing is not limited to only kindergartners and early first-grade students. Many of the Writing strand's subcategories focus on publishing writing, and we all know that most student-created texts reflect the type of texts to which they are exposed. Students often include illustrations, graphic aids, or photos in their written projects. Even at the third-grade level, students are encouraged to include illustrations, when useful, to help the reader understand the story (W.3.2). Whether students use drawing because they are just beginning to write or they use drawing to extend their writing, we should encourage the use of student-created visuals with all of our students.

What Are Some Key Themes in the ELA CCSS Writing Strand?

When we read through all of the skills and standards associated with the Writing strand in the ELA CCSS, we see many common themes. First, collaboration is important. Students are involved in collaborating with peers as they pursue ideas and get those ideas down on paper. Next, as previously mentioned, narrative writing is included in the standards, but the majority of writing standards are focused on text that communicates information. This is the type of writing that students need to be successful after formal schooling ends. Finally, we are required to help students use technology to produce and publish their writing.

Collaboration

Similar to real life, where scientists and historians collaborate to conduct research and gather information, write reports or proposals, and publish their findings, the writing students engage in to meet the ELA CCSS often requires collaboration. This is true not only for kindergartners, but also for first graders to work with peers to conduct research, strengthen writing, and publish texts. Therefore, the writing tasks we ask students to complete must encourage collaboration with other students.

Types of Writing

The text types and purposes in the ELA CCSS Writing strand vary. Beginning in kindergarten, students are expected to express their opinion through a combination of drawing, dictating, and writing and later are expected to be able to articulate in writing not only their opinion but also their reasons for the opinion (W.K.l; W.1.1; W.2.1; W.3.1). Anyone who has been around young children realizes they have strong opinions. They can debate and argue why they should or should not do something with any adult. I am sure I am not the only person who has heard from a teacher that my child should be a lawyer. However, the key is getting young children to express their views in writing. A common belief in the past was that elementary students could orally express opinions but would have difficulty writing persuasively. The reality is more than likely that rarely are elementary students writing this genre or any genre beyond narrative (Duke, 2000; Pappas, 2006). It also appears that persuasive writing rarely has been taught at the elementary grades (Anderson, 2008). Therefore, we must help students to express their opinions through writing and support their beliefs.

Along with composing pieces showing an opinion, K–3 students are expected to be able to write informational/explanatory texts. Although the writing expectations increase as students get older, the youngest literacy learners need to have an understanding of informational/explanatory texts.

Finally, students must be able to write narratives. Whereas kindergartners and first-grade students are expected only to sequence events, second- and third-grade students are expected to use dialogue and description of actions or to show a character's reaction to a situation. The depth and breadth of writing required by the ELA CCSS standards for K–3 learners means we must find a way to emphasize a wide range of writing tasks. By connecting students' writing with content area topics, we will be able to meet all of the ELA CCSS more easily because we will have stronger writers and more content-knowledgeable students.

Using Technology

We talk about preparing our students to be successful in life, and part of that requires being technologically literate so that they can contribute in a digital society (Leu, Kinzer, Coiro, & Cammack, 2004). Let's think about how the job market has changed since we were in school. Research published by the U.S. Department of Labor (2000) showed that the top five fastest growing occupations were computer engineers, computer support specialists, systems analysts, database administrators, and desktop publishing specialists. Technology use has increased since then, so the emphasis placed on preparing our students to be technologically literate should also increase.

For many digital immigrants, this is scary. However, we need to remember that we don't need to know everything about every digital tool in order to use the tools (Yuan, 2011). Children aren't born with their knowledge of technology, but many can use a smartphone or a tablet better than a lot of adults can. Children aren't afraid to take risks with technology, and they develop their knowledge by using it. There are a lot of websites out there designed for classroom use. The following are a few ideas for incorporating technology into the classroom at no cost:

- Blogging—If you are thinking about having your students create secure blogs without any advertising, consider kidblog.org/home. As a teacher, you retain control of the blogs, and there are no student e-mail accounts needed.
- Creating a class website—If you want to create a free classroom website to keep your students' parents informed about their literacy activities and content area learning, you might consider Weebly.com.

- Writing texts—StoryJumper.com is a neat website where students can create their own texts. Students can select props and scenes for their texts or upload photos that remain private. I have seen this website recommended for narrative writing, but it could be used for any type of writing and also to strengthen the literacy and content area connection.
- Expressing opinions—At Voki.com, students can select an avatar, customize the character, add voice, or upload text, and then post the avatar to their blog. Once the avatar is created, students can hone their writing skills by creating persuasive pieces and sharing these opinions through their talking avatar.

Technology can help us shape our students' writing skills. To meet the ELA CCSS, K–3 students will need to write about more than just their own ideas and knowledge. They will need to be able to conduct research, analyze the information they find, collaborate with peers, and write for a variety of purposes. To do this, students must be provided with easy access to online research sources and suggestions for digital writing and editing tools. As our students use digital tools to create and publish their written products, we are not only incorporating technology into the writing curriculum, but also enriching our students' content knowledge.

TRY IT OUT

Over a one-week period, list on a chart the types of writing in which your students participate. On it, be sure to include the content area topic targeted, the students' purpose for writing, the audience they targeted, and other important information. At the end of the week, reread and reflect on your findings. Are students demonstrating variety in each of the areas mentioned? Are they writing across the curriculum for a variety of people and creating a range of texts? Was technology incorporated into the writing? If you are not happy with the findings, rethink some of the classroom writing activities you have planned for the future. If possible, try to do this activity on a regular basis.

Everyone Gains From Writing

Writing helps students not only to become better writers, but also to develop a deeper understanding of material (Knipper & Duggan, 2006). As students write, their thinking becomes visible (Miller & Calfee, 2004). Thinking about a topic and writing about it requires a much higher level of thought than merely reading (Fordham, Wellman, & Sandman, 2002). Although students can read passively, they have to be actively involved when writing. Through writing, students realize which content area concepts they understand and what information they are still struggling to comprehend.

Students are not the only ones who can gain through writing-to-learn assignments. Teachers, too, can learn a great deal about students' knowledge by reading and discussing writing samples. Minilessons can be taught to a small group of students who are experiencing difficulty with a concept. Teachers can keep writing samples throughout the year to document students' writing growth, which is something that teachers love to see. Students are equally proud to see what and how much they have learned.

Differentiating Writing Instruction

Whether we are working with struggling readers and writers, English learners, or gifted and talented students, we need to informally assess their writing skills and provide appropriate, differentiated instruction to move them forward. The beauty of writing is that progress can be seen easily by both the teacher and the student writer. As we work with K–3 students and keep their dated artifacts, we can use the progress shown with these artifacts to encourage students to remain enthusiastic, confident, and passionate about their writing

As we work with English learners, we can expect to make additional accommodations to ensure their success with writing. These students will need more time and practice with writing assignments than their classmates (Goldenberg, 2008). In addition, we know that English learners reap many more benefits from activities that actively involve their family. Writing activities such as Getting the Message Home, which is discussed later in this chapter, can help to connect learning within the classroom to students' home setting. Any way we can modify writing assignments to involve parents, guardians, or others in the home can be beneficial to all students and specifically to English learners.

Furthermore, many teachers integrate technology with writing instruction through the use of word processing. Although all students enjoy and benefit from its usage, research suggests that students who encounter difficulties with writing can benefit from word processing specifically. Morphy and Graham (2012) reviewed 27 studies that examined the use of word processing with weak writers and readers in grades 1–12. Their review found that word processing is beneficial for struggling readers and writers. The length of the written product, organization of the content, and overall quality improved. Furthermore, students were more motivated to write when they used word processing. The fact that there are affective as well as academic benefits of using word processing programs with struggling writers makes the use of technology during writing instruction an important consideration.

Similar to reading, students will improve their writing only if they continue to write. We have to think about any specific accommodations that might help individual students to be successful writers and provide opportunities for them to participate in authentic activities that will prepare them for future writing. Providing meaningful writing activities can offer additional gains. Research (Daniels, Zemelman, & Steineke, 2007) suggests that students can retain 70% of the content information they learn if they write about it and that even greater benefits are seen when students write and talk about the content. With benefits such as these, we must work to ensure that all students can participate in quality writing experiences. Our role as educators is to provide the necessary support needed, quality writing experiences, and a commitment to nurture students' interests and abilities.

Activities for Enhancing Students' Writing Skills

Through the following activities, students are engaged in writing for a variety of purposes and audiences. They create science notebooks, informational texts, opinion pieces, and even poetry. These activities can be used across the content areas. As students have the opportunity to experience choice and extend their writing beyond the classroom, it is hoped that they will realize the enjoyment that can come from writing and learn even more about content area topics.

Taking Control of Text Features

The best way to demystify text features with young students is to introduce the features and allow students to use the features in their own writing. In this activity, the informational text has a purpose and an authentic audience, and students conduct research collaboratively to gain answers to questions they want to answer. This activity reinforces linguistic features and other elements of informational text, and also helps students to improve their writing skills.

How It Works

1. As a class, keep track of the linguistic features seen in informational text. This might be done over the course of a week or after three to five informational texts have been shared in the content areas. Students may encounter labeled diagrams, page numbers, maps and keys, tables of contents, appendixes, captions, headings, subheadings, timelines, tables, graphs, flowcharts, bold print, glossaries, and indexes. Explain to students that they will be creating a text about their school. This text will be available in the school office when new students enroll or it might be available to read during the period when kindergartners register for the next school year.

2. As a class, brainstorm and create eight questions a student might have about the school. List those questions on a chart, the document camera, or the interactive whiteboard. Read through the questions together. Questions might include Who is the principal? When does school start? Do I wear a uniform? Do I eat at school? Will I play outside? What will I learn? Will I take a nap? How will I get to school?

3. Talk about how students can find the answers to the questions. Write these suggestions next to each question. Students might talk to other students, look in books, interview adults, or review a printed text or digital text. Some types of research will be more appropriate than others for specific questions.

4. Allow students to work in small groups to find the answer to one of the questions. Each group will need a piece of paper with their specific question written on it. Students can draw a picture for the answer, write a few words, or dictate their answer. The purpose is to introduce the idea

of research and allow students to experience working in groups or with a partner to collect information on a topic.

5. Bring the class back together for students to share their answers to the questions. The answers can be written in a sentence or two underneath each question on the chart.

6. Ask students what the cover of their book should include. Think about an appropriate title for the book and the purpose of a title. Perhaps the students will want to use a photo or a drawing of the school. This might even be a good time to introduce students to using copyright-free clip art of a school building or a group of students. After the cover is created, talk about the concept of author and illustrator. List the class as author and illustrator. Then talk about the copyright date of the text, and why it is important with informational text.

7. Create pages for the book. The heading for each page (written in a different color and font than the text) might be one of the questions posed by the class. A photo, diagram, or chart can be added along with a sentence or two that provides the answer to the question. This is a good time to discuss the type of information students want to include in the text and to help them understand when a graph, drawing, or photo might be the most appropriate visual for conveying information. Also, share why students might want the heading to be written in a different color and font than the rest of the text. Refer to texts that students have read that include some of the linguistic features they are using in their text. For example, students may interview the bus driver, principal, or other students to learn about ways people get to school. Then students can write a sentence such as, "Students get to school by bus, car, walking, and taxis." With this information, students may decide they want to create a pie graph showing how kindergartners get to school.

8. After the text is created, ask students why they created the book about their school. Show an example of a text where the author shares the reason behind the creation of the text. Put this information on a page called Author's Purpose.

9. Reread the text with students. Ask them if there are any key terms that they think readers may need to know before reading the text. Determine the best way for readers to find the meaning for the terms. Perhaps students can create a glossary for the book.

10. As a class, add a page number at the bottom of each page. Then create a table of contents for the front of the book. Talk about why it is important to have a table of contents and page numbers in an informational text. Do those features make it easier for readers to find information quickly?

Additional Suggestions

You can easily modify this activity for use with slightly older students by decreasing the amount and type of scaffolding provided. Perhaps the students can create a text about their town and send it to a class in another state or country. A book on a specific city or town might include the following questions: Where is the town located? What fun activities are there? What festivals are there? What is the climate? Where do people live? What types of food are popular to eat? Students might be able to write out the answers to their questions and decide with their peers on the type of visual aid that is most appropriate for each question. Photos of dwellings such as apartments, public housing, duplexes, and hotels may be the best way to talk about types of housing. Much of the research and writing can be completed on the computer. The most important thing to remember is that students need an authentic audience. They need to think about what the audience might know about the topic and what information would be important to share with the audience.

Psst! Did You Know?

In this activity, students are introduced to an award-winning informational text and have an opportunity to use some of the techniques in that text to create their own informational text. This activity is designed to be completed early in the school year, and it gives students a chance to participate in a fun project for sharing information about their classroom with their parents. Students can try to complete the book prior to the school's open house.

There are many mentor texts that can be used for this activity. I chose *Life-Size Zoo* (Komiya, 2008) because the text contains unique features. My hope is that students will enjoy a quality text and that the activity will develop "feature consciousness." Similar to word consciousness, I want students to develop an awareness and interest in features that authors use to create informational texts.

How It Works

1. Share *Life-Size Zoo* with your students. This wonderful text is a recipient of the Parents' Choice Gold Award and introduces a variety of animals to students. The animals on the pages are actual size. This means for very large animals only part of the body is shown. Ask students what they think is meant by the title. Before reading the text, have students look at the way the author sets up the table of contents. In this book, the sequence of the pages is not important, so the author made the table of contents resemble a zoo map. The students can discuss the positives and negatives of the table of contents page. (For example, one negative is that the table of contents makes it more difficult to find a particular animal in the text.)

2. As a class, read through the book once. Tell students that you are going to read through the book again, and you want them to tell you if they notice anything special or unique about the book. How does the author share information? How are the pages set up? You may need to draw their attention to certain items. Students will note that the topic represented on each page is shown in large font. There is usually a sentence about the topic on the opposite page. A life-size photo takes up both pages. Students will also notice that details for the topic are given in a small column on the right-hand side of every page. (A few pages open up further, but unless large sheets of drawing paper are available for those pages, it won't be possible to recreate that stylistic device.)

3. Tell students that they are going to create a book about their class. Kindergartners and first graders may create a whole-class text while older students may be able to create individual texts. Students can share the books with a family member so that they know more about their classroom. If a class book is created, send home a letter to the parents letting them know that a very important text will be coming home. Emphasize the importance of returning the book promptly and keeping it safe from younger siblings' hands so that all families can enjoy it. You might consider having parents sign the letter prior to the text being sent home so that you know the adults are expecting it. Include a note with the book reiterating guidelines. Put the book, the note, and an empty journal in a large resealable plastic bag before sending it home. After parents read the text, they can write a note to the class about the book. Students will enjoy reading the feedback parents provide in the journal. If it is unlikely that

every family will return it, a color copy of the original text might be made and the original retained.

4. Discuss an appropriate title for the text. Although *Life-Size Zoo* may feel appropriate for the classroom some days, I would suggest *Life-Size Classroom* or a similar title. Ask students what topics they might want to include in their books. The topics contain one or two words and are set in a large font on the page. List students' ideas on the chalkboard. Students will probably want pages that share information about you as their teacher, their classmates, where they eat lunch, what technology is available (e.g., computers, tablets, smartboards), any special areas (e.g., physical education, art, music), a class pet, and other topics.

5. As a class, discuss the creation of one page. Perhaps start with the page about the teacher. Together, talk about how students can mimic the mentor text *Life-Size Zoo*. They will want to put *Teacher* in a large font on the left-hand side of the page. Then students will want to write a sentence about you as their teacher on the right. It will be a short sentence similar to the mentor text, such as "Mrs. Roberts is our third-grade teacher." Students might also choose to trace your "life-size" hand holding a piece of chalk as the picture for the page. Then students should think of fun facts they might list or draw about you in a column on the right-hand side of the page. These facts could include "This is her fifth year teaching," "She has a dog named Rupert" (complete with a drawing of the dog), and "Her favorite color is blue." Similarly, for a page about school lunch, students may decide to put the word *Lunch* in bold font and then write a sentence sharing that they eat in the lunchroom. Students might trace a life-size carton of milk they drink at lunch. Then they can include fun facts about their lunch. Perhaps they always have pizza on Friday or get an ice cream on Monday.

6. After discussing the manner in which students might create a page about their teacher, review the other brainstormed topics. Have students share what life-size picture they might include for an illustration for each topic. That concept will probably be the hardest for young students to determine. Even if they can't put a life-size tablet or smartboard on their page, they could trace a life-size computer mouse or draw a few life-size keys.

7. Before students get started, skim through the text and list a few key features you want students to include in their book. This might include the

topic listed in bold, large font, a life-size illustration representing the topic, and two or three fun facts in a column on the right-hand side of the page.

8. Allow students to work with partners or individually to create their texts.

9. Have a book sharing with the texts before they go home to the families.

Think Like a Scientist!

This activity was created by Nesbit, Hargrove, Harrelson, and Maxey (2004) so that students in even the lowest grades could create science notebooks. Through the use of science notebooks, teachers can better understand student thinking and reinforce the way scientists keep records. As students ask questions about the world around them and seek answers, they realize that they are already scientists. Our little scientists need a place to document their scientific findings. A science notebook is ideal. With our youngest students, we will need to adapt the activity to meet their needs, and we may even model and create a class folder that serves as a science notebook. This type of writing is more similar to the type of record keeping and writing that we see with the scientific method than journal writing that is much more open ended. Although journals are popular in K–3 classrooms, we want to think about our goal when selecting writing activities.

How It Works

1. Orally share informational texts such as *What Is a Scientist?* (Lehn, 1999) and *Scientists Ask Questions* (Garrett, 2005) with students. Then discuss with the class what it means to be a scientist and keep scientific records. Do they know any scientists? Are they ready to become scientists?

2. Plan a simple experiment that ties to their science content. Students learning about plants might decide to grow three identical plants but modify their treatment. One plant might get sunlight and water. One may get sunlight and orange juice, and one might be given sunlight and no liquid. This is an excellent time to reinforce that students only want to change one variable. If they choose to put one of the plants in the dark, they won't know whether it is the lack of sunlight or the liquid (or lack of) that influenced plant growth. Ask students to think of as many questions as they

can about plants. Help them to revise one of those questions into one that can be investigated. This question might be, Do plants need water to grow?

3. Introduce the class science notebook. You might create this by stapling together 5–10 sheets of large paper. Write the name of the class, the date, and the time in the top corner of the first sheet. Then write the question students created at the top of that same sheet.

4. On the next page, write "Prediction." Ask students to tell you what they think will happen. List their predictions on the page.

5. Discuss the materials needed for students to answer the question. On a new page, write "Materials Needed" and list those items.

6. Gather the materials and conduct the experiment.

7. On a new page, write "What We Did." You might encourage students to orally list a couple of steps that were completed or to draw a picture to show what was done. This is a good time to reinforce the fact that there are many types of writing. Writing steps requires students to be concise and to write in a specific sequence that can be followed. Diagrams are another way to share information with readers, but you must label a diagram's parts to help the audience understand what is being shown.

8. Then write "Results." In this area, students state in a sentence or two what happened as a result of the experiment.

9. Talk about science notebooks. Why is it important for scientists to keep records such as these? How is this type of writing different from other types of writing students do in class? What other experiments might they conduct? Depending on the students, it may be possible for them to complete a science notebook entry on their own with scaffolding from you. However, by completing the science notebook as a class, even the youngest learners can begin to think like scientists.

The Choice Is Theirs

As discussed earlier in this book, we know that choice is powerful. This strategy can be implemented with almost any type of writing assignment, but we want to ensure that students experience a wide range of writing. Therefore, we need to keep track of student writing. A chart may work best for record keeping. The students may even keep a copy of the chart in a notebook. Although students have a choice in the type of writing they do, the next time The Choice Is Theirs they will need to select a type of writing not done before.

This activity should be used after students have been introduced to the diverse forms of writing. For a class of young students who may be completing very different types of writing activities to have choice, they will need more guidance than one teacher can provide. Therefore, this activity can serve as an excellent way to bridge the grade levels. After being mentored on how to best assist younger students, older students can help them complete their work. Older students will also gain from the collaboration with younger students (Hickey & DeCoste, 1998). They will develop additional experience collaborating with others, including those much younger; they will have an opportunity to explore a topic in depth about which they may not possess a great deal of knowledge; and they will gain additional literacy skills as they help younger students write for a variety of purposes.

How It Works

1. Determine the writing topic. Perhaps it is recycling.

2. Brainstorm the types of writing students might complete that relate to the topic. The following are examples that tie to recycling:

- Create a flowchart showing what happens when someone puts a can in a recycling bin.
- Write an opinion piece offering three reasons why recycling is important.
- Write a narrative story about how their family does or does not recycle. Encourage the use of temporal words to signify order. Who is involved with recycling in their family? If the family doesn't recycle, what happens to the cans, paper, and so forth? What are their feelings related to recycling? The students' job isn't to persuade anyone. This is just a narrative on their experiences with the topic.
- Write an informational piece outlining the steps to recycle. Do containers need to be cleaned or modified in any way before they go in the recycling bin? Where do people get the recycling bins? What do people do with the recycling bins once they are full?

- Draw a poster showing all the materials that can be recycled where they live and label each item. Remind students of the importance of a header or title for the poster.

3. After all of the ideas for writing are brainstormed, ask students who they expect to be the audience for their work. Encourage students to think of people other than their teacher as the audience for their work.

4. Brainstorm the various ways that students might locate the information needed for their writing. Gather informational books, share websites, Skype with an employee at a local recycling plant, or take a virtual field trip to a recycling plant. There are many options.

5. When the students have finished their writing projects, they can determine how they want to share the information they learned. Again, the choice is theirs. Students can be videotaped while they read their writing, and the video can be posted using a private link on YouTube or it may be shared on the school morning news program or on the class website. Posters or diagrams might be displayed in the hallways as part of the school's local text. Narrative stories can be combined to create a text that can be given to another class for its classroom library or read to a class at a lower grade level.

6. Afterward, have students discuss what they wrote, the audience, and the manner in which it was shared. Also, talk about the types of writing students might want to do the next time The Choice Is Theirs! Young students might want to keep doing the same type of writing, so explain why it is important to try other types. That doesn't mean they can't create another diagram, but there are many interesting types of writing they can do.

Getting the Message Home

We are always looking for ways students can write for authentic audiences. Creating family message journals serves that purpose. Wollman-Bonilla (2001) states, "Because messages are related to classroom activities families do not experience, they are a genuine communication of ideas, knowledge, and needs unknown to the intended reader" (p. 187) and emphasizes that teachers never write in these journals. Through family message journals, students can improve their writing-to-learn skills as they engage in making powerful connections with content area material.

How It Works

1. Before starting this activity, send a note home to parents or guardians explaining the purpose of the family message journal. Explain when the journal will be sent home, the type of response desired, and the necessity of returning the journal. Discuss the importance of the journal and the benefits of students' involvement with it.

2. Explain to students that they are going to share what they are learning in math, science, and social studies with their family in a family message journal. Begin by providing materials and letting students create their journal covers, making sure to include a title.

3. Remind students that their families do not know what they are learning in class so they need to be detailed in their writing to help their family understand. Any adult can read and respond: an older sibling, an aunt, a grandparent, or a neighbor or friend of the family if necessary. Decide on the topic for the students' first journal entry. What have they been learning in the content areas? The following are some examples of the type of entries that might be included in the family message journals (our youngest students can draw pictures as part of their entry):

- An opinion entry on why recycling is important
- A how-to entry that sequences how students conducted a science experiment and what they learned from it
- An informational entry explaining what students are learning in math
- A descriptive entry about the garden the class planted
- An entry that tells about a field trip students may be planning, why they are going, and what they hope to learn

4. After students decide on the journal topic, it is time to start writing. Remind students to think of their audience and what information is important to share. Because the students are young, it is easiest to have everyone write the same type of entry. That way, you can model and emphasize the type of writing students will be doing. The steps to a science experiment will be written differently from an opinion piece on recycling or a description of their class garden.

5. If possible, photocopy the written journal entry. This doesn't need to be done every time, but these artifacts can serve as an informal assessment of the students' writing skills. It will also help to keep a list of the type of writing the students are engaging with in the journal. In doing so, you ensure that a variety of writing is being taught. The family message journals reinforce many types of writing that are included in the ELA CCSS writing standards.

Sharing My Opinion

Anyone who has spent any time around children is well aware that they have opinions. In the past, we rarely required very young learners to share their opinions in writing. The ELA CCSS require that children as young as kindergarten age start learning how to share their views in writing.

In fact, argumentation is considered a key focus of the ELA CCSS. Helping students learn to express their opinions is a step in helping them to take a position on a topic. This activity will help students learn to express opinions in writing and to critically listen, view, and read texts in which the author or creator may be trying to persuade them. We all know that students are constantly surrounded by persuasive text: Watch a children's television show, and you will see how advertisers try to convince young viewers that they need the latest toy. Persuasive text is text that shares an opinion but goes one step further to try to convince readers that the opinion expressed in the text is the best opinion.

How It Works

1. Talk about what it means to express an opinion. Can someone express an opinion and make someone think or act a certain way? Bring in examples of snack boxes or show short video clips of toy commercials that appeal to children. What about those texts makes them interested in the food or toys? Explain that texts are often written to get people, even children, to think a certain way.

2. Ask students what they liked best about their last thematic unit in science or social studies. Perhaps it was the field trip they took, the experiment they conducted, or the books that were shared. If students recently completed a unit on plants, the opinion statement may be, "The best part of our thematic unit was planting the garden." The following are other

topics that tie to the content areas that students might choose to write about. They are not meant to be sentence starters but to provide additional suggestions for writing:

- The best place to live is _____.
- The scariest type of animal is _____.
- The best type of plant is _____.
- The greatest invention is _____.
- The most important sense is _____.
- _____ is one of the greatest people to ever live.

3. Explain to students that it is their turn to persuade someone else with their writing. If students are kindergartners or beginning first graders, it might work best to create a whole-class text.

4. Start by asking students who they are persuading. For this basic example, it may not matter whether students identify their parents, their classmates, or a teacher. It simply helps young children to realize that an author must consider an audience when writing. Ask the students to select a topic and state their opinion in one sentence. Model sentences for the students so they understand the expectations. Then write the sentence at the top of a sheet of paper.

5. As a class, discuss how writers support their arguments or opinions with reasons. One narrative text I love to share that illustrates the importance of supporting an argument is *Hey Little Ant!* (Hoose, Hoose, & Tilley, 1998). Although it is not an informational book, it provides an excellent example of a young boy and ants arguing for and against why ants shouldn't be squished. Children can relate to the story, and the illustrations will draw them into the dilemma. After sharing this book, draw a line down a sheet of paper. Write "Boy" at the top of the left side and "Ants" at the top of the right side. Go back through the text to see if the students can find the reasoning given to support the opinions of both sides and list the arguments in the appropriate column.

6. Now look at the topic statement on which the students will write. Ask the students to give you three to five reasons that support their opinion sentence. Why do they feel a certain way about the topic? If students are able, ask them to use other sources to get additional supporting ideas. They may ask an adult to help them to search online, skim through an

informational text, or take an informal poll to see if others agree. Have students complete the Sharing My Opinion Sheet on page 168 in the Appendix. For example, students may decide that their topic is "How We Get to School." Their audience is their parents. Students may state their opinion as "It is best to walk to school." Their reasons could be that walking saves money because parents don't need to buy as much gas for the car, provides students with exercise, keeps parents from needing to find the car keys in the morning, allows students to get to school faster because they can walk through yards instead of using the streets, and allows students to leave earlier after school than those riding the buses.

7. Have students combine the sentences to write a persuasive text. Then let them share their text with their classmates. As students listen, see if the author is able to give reasons for the opinion stated, and ask other students what reasons they hear mentioned in the text.

Poems for Multiple Voices

Writing poetry is a great way to encourage students to discuss content area information. Once students move beyond their initial belief that all poetry rhymes, they will find the task much easier. In Poems for Multiple Voices, students can compare and contrast information on two related content area topics. They will not only be discussing content area information, but also using higher level thinking as they look for similarities and differences on two topics.

How It Works

1. Explain to students that they are going to create a poem showing two or more views on a topic. If possible, share a poem from one of Mary Ann Hoberman's (2001, 2004) books, such as *You Read to Me, I'll Read to You: Very Short Stories to Read Together* or *You Read to Me, I'll Read to You: Very Short Fairy Tales to Read Together*, which use color coding to differentiate the voices.

2. Select a topic. For kindergartners, it may be something as simple as a season such as winter. Then talk about how animals may view winter very differently. For very young children, you may have to help them

156

come up with two types of animals. What do these animals do in the winter?

3. In the middle of a smartboard, write the title of the poem. In this example, the title may be "Winter." Then write *Birds* at the top of the left side of the board and *Bears* at the top of the right side. Is there anything about winter on which both birds and bears may agree? Students may say, "It is cold." List that and any other ideas in a column in the middle of the board.

4. Ask students to give you some opinions or facts that are specific to the topic. What do birds do in winter? When an idea is given, ask the students for a matching idea that applies to bears. What do bears do in winter? List all ideas under the appropriate columns. The beginning of a kindergarten class poem on winter may look like this:

Winter

Birds		Bears
	Winter is cold.	
	We change our behavior.	
Most of us fly south to warm weather.		We plan ahead and hibernate until the weather warms up.

The poem can continue with other suggestions provided by students.

A Look Inside One Classroom

A group of second-grade students were reviewing animal groups. They brainstormed 29 animals and organized them into one of the six main animal groups studied at their grade level: reptiles, insects, birds, fish, amphibians, and mammals. If students were unsure how to categorize any animal they brainstormed, they searched online for an answer. Then the teacher asked them what two animal groups they would like to compare and contrast. The class chose mammals and reptiles.

The class brainstormed how the two animal groups were different. Students' ideas were listed in the appropriate column on a large sheet of paper:

Mammals	Reptiles
Mammals nurse their babies.	Reptiles have their babies in eggs.
Mammals have hair.	Reptiles have rough, scaly skin.
Mammals have a backbone.	Reptiles (snakes) shed their exoskeleton.

After looking at each pair of statements, students came up with a sentence showing how both groups were the same. Those sentences were added to the paper in the middle column, resulting in the following poem:

Mammals   Reptiles

Mammals nurse their babies.

                                            Reptiles have their babies in eggs.

                  Animals take care of their babies.

Mammals have hair.

                                              Reptiles have rough, scaly skin.

                  Hair and skin keep animals warm.

Mammals have a backbone.

                                            Reptiles (snakes) shed their exoskeleton.

                  Animals are on the move.

Afterward, students decided on a title for their poem. They initially thought "Mammals and Reptiles are Alike and Different" would be the title but decided "Amazing Animal Groups" was a better title to describe their poem. The class then read chorally the poem. Poems for Multiple Voices is a versatile activity that can be used easily with a variety of content area topics. It not only provides an excellent opportunity for students to write to learn, but it also engages them in comparing and contrasting content from content area topics studied in class.

REFLECTING BACK AS WE MOVE FORWARD

Writing is a valuable skill that we must foster in our earliest literacy learners because they will need to be able write proficiently the rest of their lives. Young children often come to us knowing very little about using words for writing, but some may like to imitate parents making lists and writing notes. We must encourage this interest and enthusiasm in writing so that they continue to want to write. By providing appropriate scaffolding, we can help our students to be prepared for the writing demands they will encounter in later grades and in life. Students are expected to be able to present an argument, write an informational piece, and create a narrative story through visuals and words. The only way we can move them toward this goal is through creating powerful connections between literacy and the content areas.

Reproducibles

TEXT IS ALL AROUND ME CHART

Name _____

Text Is All Around Me

Date	Text	Where Was It Seen?	Why Did You Read the Text?	Did Anyone Read It With You?

TEXT IS ALL AROUND ME—
LETTER TO PARENTS AND GUARDIANS

Today's Date _____

Dear Parent or Guardian:

In class, we are learning the importance of text, and that text is everywhere. I would like to ask your help with this activity. Attached to this letter is a sheet titled Text Is All Around Me. With your help, I would like to have students keep track of any text they read outside of the classroom. It might work best to fill in the chart each evening or twice a day on weekends so that none of the text read is forgotten.

Text is a broad term. It can include stories (make believe and nonfiction), newspapers, advertising circulars, cereal boxes, magazines, maps, menus, postcards, recipes, instructions, signs, comics, game-related print, e-mails, Internet sites, and digital print such as computer games. Please put the date in the Date column and then list the types of text read under the column labeled Text. Also, note where the text was seen because this will help the students to realize that text truly is everywhere. Under the Why Did You Read the Text? column, write why the text was read. If it is a bedtime story, the text might have been read for fun. If the text is a flier about a movie, a note about softball practice, a postcard from a relative, or directions on a cake box, the text most likely will have been read for information. This allows students to realize that we read for a wide variety of reasons. Finally, if your child was involved with others when reading the text, write that in the last column.

Thank you so much for taking the time to make sure that the Text Is All Around Me sheet is completed and returned to class. It is important for children to realize that text plays an important role in their lives both inside and outside the classroom. If you have any questions, please let me know. I would like the sheet returned on _____.

Sincerely yours,

_____

LINGUISTIC FEATURES CHART

Topic _____

FEATURES	BOOK 1	BOOK 2	BOOK 3	BOOK 4
Appendix				
Captions				
Electronic Menus				
Flowcharts				
Fonts				
Glossary				
Graphs				
Headings/Subheadings				
Hyperlinks				
Icons				
Index				
Labeled Diagrams				
Maps and Keys				
Sidebars				
Table of Contents				
Tables				
Timelines				

Book 1 _____

Book 2 _____

Book 3 _____

Book 4 _____

CONTENT AREA TRADE BOOK EVALUATION

Scoring: 1 = does not meet expectations; 3 = meets expectations; 5 = exceeds expectations.

Book/Author	Accuracy of Content	Cohesion of Ideas	Organization and Layout	Specialized Vocabulary	Student Considerations	Teacher Goals
	Outstanding Features:					
	Outstanding Features:					
	Outstanding Features:					
	Outstanding Features:					

TEXT COMPLEXITY CHART

TOPIC/THEME _____

1. TEXT/AUTHOR _____

GENRE
LITERATURE   NONFICTION
                 INFO.   OTHER

NUMBER OF WORDS

EASE OF LANGUAGE
Figurative   Word Choice

PRESENTATION OF INFORMATION
Linguistic Features   Organization   Visuals

COMMENTS:

2. TEXT/AUTHOR _____

GENRE
LITERATURE   NONFICTION
                 INFO.   OTHER

NUMBER OF WORDS

EASE OF LANGUAGE
Figurative   Word Choice

PRESENTATION OF INFORMATION
Linguistic Features   Organization   Visuals

COMMENTS:

3. TEXT/AUTHOR _____

GENRE
LITERATURE   NONFICTION
                 INFO.   OTHER

NUMBER OF WORDS

EASE OF LANGUAGE
Figurative   Word Choice

PRESENTATION OF INFORMATION
Linguistic Features   Organization   Visuals

COMMENTS:

P = Positive   N = Negative

ABC+ BRAINSTORMING SHEET

	Brainstorm	Other Ideas
A		
B		
C		
D		
E		
F		
G		
H		
I		
J		
K		
L		
M		
N		
O		
P		
Q		
R		
S		
T		
U		
V		
W		
X		
Y		
Z		

VOCABULARY VISIT: BEFORE THE VISIT SHEET

Name _____

Topic _____

BEFORE THE VISIT
SHOW WHAT YOU KNOW!

These Are Some Words That I Know!

_____   _____

_____   _____

_____   _____

_____   _____

_____   _____

Note. From Vocabulary Visits: Virtual Field Trips for Content Vocabulary Development, by C.L.Z. Blachowicz and C. Obrochta, 2005, *The Reading Teacher, 59,* p. 265. Copyright 2005 by the International Reading Association. Adapted with permission.

VOCABULARY VISIT: AFTER THE VISIT SHEET

Name _____

Topic _____

<u>AFTER THE VISIT</u>
SHOW WHAT YOU KNOW!

Look How Many Words I Know Now!

_____   _____   _____

_____   _____   _____

_____   _____   _____

_____   _____   _____

_____   _____   _____

SHARING MY OPINION SHEET

Name _____

Topic _____

Audience "The Who?" _____

Reasons

Opinion

REFERENCES

Allington, R.L. (1984). Content coverage and contextual reading in reading groups. *Journal of Literacy Research, 16*(2), 85–97.

Almasi, J.F. (2008). Using questioning strategies to promote students' active discussion and comprehension of content area material. In D. Lapp, J. Flood, & N. Farnan (Eds.), *Content area reading and learning* (3rd ed., pp. 487–513). New York, NY: Erlbaum.

Altieri, J.L. (2010). *Literacy + math = Creative connections in the elementary classroom.* Newark, DE: International Reading Association.

Altieri, J.L. (2011). *Content counts! Developing disciplinary literacy skills, K–6.* Newark, DE: International Reading Association.

Alvermann, D.E. (2001). *Effective literacy instruction for adolescents.* Executive summary and paper commissioned by the National Reading Conference. Chicago, IL.

Anderson, D.D. (2008). The elementary persuasive letter: Two cases of situated competence, strategy, and agency. *Research in the Teaching of English, 42*(3), 270–314.

Atkinson, T.S., Matusevich, M.N., & Huber, L. (2009). Making science trade book choices for elementary classrooms. *The Reading Teacher, 62*(6), 484–497.

Avery, C. (2003). Nonfiction books: Naturals for the primary level. In R.A. Bamford & J.V. Kristo (Eds.), *Making facts come alive: Choosing and using nonfiction literature K–8* (2nd ed., pp. 235–246). Norwood, MA: Christopher-Gordon.

Avgerinou, M.D. (2009). Re-viewing visual literacy in the "bain d'images" era. *TechTrends, 53*(2), 28–34.

Baker, S.K., Gersten, R., Haager, D., & Dingle, M. (2006). Teaching practice and the reading growth of first-grade English learners: Validation of an observation instrument. *The Elementary School Journal, 107*(2), 199–219.

Bamford, R.A., Kristo, J.V., & Lyon, A. (2002). Facing facts: Nonfiction in the primary classroom. *The New England Reading Association Journal, 38*(2), 8–15.

Beach, R., & Myers, J. (2001). *Inquiry-based English instruction: Engaging students in life and literature.* New York, NY: Teachers College Press.

Bear, D.R., Helman, L., Templeton, S., Invernizzi, M., & Johnston, F. (2007). *Words their way with English learners: Word study for phonics, vocabulary, and spelling instruction.* Upper Saddle River, NJ: Pearson Prentice Hall.

Beck, I.L., McKeown, M.G., & Kucan, L. (2002). *Bringing words to life: Robust vocabulary instruction.* New York, NY: Guilford.

Best, R.M., Floyd, R.G., & McNamara, D.S. (2008). Differential competencies contributing to children's comprehension of narrative and expository texts. *Reading Psychology, 29*(2), 137–164.

Biemiller, A. (2004). Teaching vocabulary in the primary grades: Vocabulary instruction needed. In J.F. Baumann & E.J. Kame'enui (Eds.), *Vocabulary instruction: Research to practice* (pp. 28–40). New York, NY: Guilford.

Biemiller, A. (2005). Size and sequence in vocabulary development: Implications for choosing words for primary grade vocabulary instruction. In E.H. Hiebert & M.L. Kamil (Eds.), *Teaching and learning vocabulary: Bringing research to practice* (pp. 227–242). Mahwah, NJ: Erlbaum.

Blachowicz, C.L.Z., & Fisher, P. (2000). Vocabulary instruction. In M.L. Kamil, P.B. Mosenthal, P.D. Pearson, & R. Barr (Eds.), *Handbook of reading research* (Vol. 3, pp. 503–524). Mahwah, NJ: Erlbaum.

Blachowicz, C.L.Z., Fisher, P.J., Ogle, D., & Watts-Taffe, S.M. (2006). Vocabulary questions from the classroom. *Reading Research Quarterly, 41*(4), 524–539.

Blachowicz, C.L.Z., & Obrochta, C. (2005). Vocabulary visits: Virtual field trips for content vocabulary development. *The Reading Teacher, 59*(3), 262–268.

Bodrova, E., & Leong, D.J. (1998). Scaffolding emergent writing in the zone of proximal development. *Literacy Teaching and Learning, 3*(2), 1–18.

Brassell, D. (2006). Inspiring young scientists with great books. *The Reading Teacher, 60*(4), 336–342.

Calderón, M., August, D., Slavin, R., Duran, D., Madden, N., & Cheung, A. (2005). Bringing words to life in classrooms with English-language learners. In E.H. Hiebert & M.L. Kamil (Eds.), *Teaching and learning vocabulary: Bringing research to practice* (pp. 117–136). Mahwah, NJ: Erlbaum.

Calhoun, E.F. (1999). *Teaching beginning reading and writing with the picture word inductive model.* Alexandria, VA: Association for Supervision and Curriculum Development.

Calo, K.M. (2011). Incorporating informational texts in the primary grades: A research-based rationale, practical strategies, and two teachers' experiences. *Early Childhood Education, 39*(4), 291–295.

Casey, B., Kersh, J.E., & Young, J.M. (2004). Storytelling sagas: An effective medium for teaching early childhood mathematics. *Early Childhood Research Quarterly, 19*(1), 167–172.

Caswell, L.J., & Duke, N.K. (1998). Non-narrative as a catalyst for literacy development. *Language Arts, 75*(2), 108–117.

Chapman, M., Filipenko, M., McTavish, M., & Shapiro, J. (2007). First graders' preferences for narrative and/or information books and perceptions of other boys' and girls' book preferences. *Canadian Journal of Education, 30*(2), 531–553.

Collard, S.B., III. (2003). Using science books to teach literacy—and save the planet. *The Reading Teacher, 57*(3), 280–283.

Colman, P. (2007). A new way to look at literature: A visual model for analyzing fiction and nonfiction texts. *Language Arts, 84*(3), 257–268.

Coltheart, M. (1979). When can children learn to read—and when should they be taught? In T.G. Waller & G.E. Mackinnon (Eds.), *Reading research: Advances in theory and practice* (Vol. 1, pp. 1–30). New York, NY: Academic.

Conley, M.W. (2008). *Content area literacy: Learners in context.* Boston, MA: Allyn & Bacon.

Connor, C.M., Kaya, S., Luck, M., Toste, J.R., Canto, A., Rice, D.,...Underwood, P.S. (2010). Content area literacy: Individualizing student instruction in second-grade science. *The Reading Teacher, 63*(6), 474–485.

Connor, C.M., Morrison, F.J., & Slominski, L. (2006). Preschool instruction and children's emergent literacy growth. *Journal of Educational Psychology, 98*(4), 665–689.

Considine, D., Horton, J., & Moorman, G. (2009). Teaching and reaching the millennial generation through media literacy. *Journal of Adolescent & Adult Literacy, 52*(6), 471–481.

Corden, R. (2007). Developing reading-writing connections: The impact of explicit instruction of literary devices on the quality of children's narrative writing. *Journal of Research in Childhood Education, 21*(3), 269–285.

Coyne, M.D., Simmons, D., & Kame'enui, E.J. (2004). Vocabulary instruction for young children at risk of experiencing reading difficulties: Teaching word meanings during shared story book reading. In J.F. Baumann & E.J. Kame'enui (Eds.), *Vocabulary instruction: Research to practice* (pp. 41–59). New York, NY: Guilford.

Cullinan, B.E. (1989). *Literature and the child* (2nd ed.). San Diego, CA: Harcourt Brace Jovanovich.

Daisey, P. (1994). The value of trade books in secondary science and mathematics instruction: A rationale. *School Science and Mathematics, 94*(3), 130–137.

Daniels, H., Zemelman, S., & Steineke, N. (2007). *Content-area writing: Every teacher's guide*. Portsmouth, NH: Heinemann.

Darling, S., & Westberg, L. (2004). Parent involvement in children's acquisition of reading. *The Reading Teacher, 57*(8), 774–776.

Donovan, C.A., & Smolkin, L.B. (2002). Considering genre, content, and visual features in the selection of trade books for science instruction. *The Reading Teacher, 55*(6), 502–520.

Douville, P. (2000). Helping parents develop literacy at home. *Preventing School Failure, 44*, 179–181.

Duke, N.K. (2000). 3.6 minutes per day: The scarcity of informational texts in first grade. *Reading Research Quarterly, 35*(2), 202–224.

Duke, N.K., & Bennett-Armistead, V.S. (2003). *Reading and writing informational text in the primary grades: Research-based practices*. New York, NY: Scholastic.

Duke, N.K., & Kays, J. (1998). "Can I say 'once upon a time'?" Kindergarten children developing knowledge of information book language. *Early Childhood Research Quarterly, 13*(2), 295–318.

Duke, N.K., & Pearson, P.D. (2002). Effective practices for developing reading comprehension. In A.E. Farstrup & S.J. Samuels (Eds.), *What research has to say about reading instruction* (pp. 205–242). Newark, DE: International Reading Association.

Duke, N.K., & Purcell-Gates, V. (2003). Genres at home and at school: Bridging the known to the new. *The Reading Teacher, 57*(1), 30–37.

Duke, N.K., Purcell-Gates, V., Hall, L.A., & Tower, C. (2006). Authentic literacy activities for developing comprehension and writing. *The Reading Teacher, 60*(4), 344–355.

Ehri, L. C., Dreyer, L. G., Flugman, B., & Gross, A. (2007). Reading Rescue: An effective tutoring intervention model for language-minority students who are struggling readers in first grade. *American Educational Research Journal, 44*(2), 414–448.

Finn, P.J. (1999). *Literacy with an attitude: Educating working-class children in their own self-interest*. Albany: State University of New York Press.

Fisher, D., Flood, J., Lapp, D., & Frey, N. (2004). Interactive read-alouds: Is there a common set of implementation practices? *The Reading Teacher, 58*(1), 8–17.

Fisher, D., & Frey, N. (2003). Writing instruction for struggling adolescent readers: A gradual release model. *Journal of Adolescent & Adult Literacy, 46*(5), 396–407.

Fisher, D., & Frey, N. (2004). *Improving adolescent literacy: Strategies that work*. Upper Saddle River, NJ: Pearson.

Fisher, D., & Frey, N. (2013). *Text complexity: Thinking about scope and sequence* [Blog post. Retrieved www.reading.org/general/Publications/blog/engage/engage-single-post/engage/2013/01/29/text-complexity-thinking-about-scope-and-sequence

Fisher, D., Frey, N., & Lapp, D. (2008). Shared readings: Modeling comprehension, vocabulary, text structures, and text features for older readers. *The Reading Teacher*, *61*(7), 548–556.

Fisher, D., Frey, N., & Lapp, D. (2012). *Text complexity: Raising rigor in reading*. Newark, DE: International Reading Association.

Flowerday, T., & Schraw, G. (2000). Teacher beliefs about instructional choice: A phenomenological study. *Journal of Education Psychology*, *92*(4), 634–645.

Flynt, E.S., & Brozo, W. (2010). Visual literacy and the content classroom: A question of now, not when. *The Reading Teacher*, *63*(6), 526–528.

Folse, K.S. (2004). *Vocabulary myths: Applying second language research to classroom teaching*. Ann Arbor: University of Michigan Press.

Fordham, N.W., Wellman, D., & Sandman, A. (2002). Taming the text: Engaging and supporting students in social studies readings. *The Social Studies*, *93*(4), 149–158.

Fountas, I., & Pinnell, G.S. (1999). *Matching books to readers: Using leveled books in guided reading, K–3*. Portsmouth, NH: Heinemann.

Gambrell, L.B. (2004). Exploring the connection between oral language and early reading. *The Reading Teacher*, *57*(5), 490–492.

Garcia, E.E., Jensen, B.T., & Scribner, K.P. (2009). The demographic imperative. *Educational Leadership*, *66*(7), 8–13.

Giblin, J.C. (2000). More than just the facts: A hundred years of children's nonfiction. *The Horn Book*, *76*(4), 413–424.

Gill, S.R. (2009). What teachers need to know about the "new" nonfiction. *The Reading Teacher*, *63*(4). 260–267.

Goldenberg, C. (2008). Teaching English language learners: What the research does—and does not—say. *American Educator*, *3*(2), 8–44.

Graves, M.F., & Watts-Taffe, S.M. (2002). The place of word consciousness in a research-based vocabulary program. In A.E. Farstrup & S.J. Samuels (Eds.), *What research has to say about reading instruction* (3rd ed., pp. 140–165). Newark, DE: International Reading Association.

Greenwood, S. (2004). Content matters: Building vocabulary and conceptual understanding in the subject areas. *Middle School Journal*, *35*(3), 27–34.

Griffin, P.L., & Olson, M.W. (1992). Phonemic awareness helps beginning readers break the code. *The Reading Teacher*, *45*(7), 516–523.

Guthrie, J.T., & Davis, M.H. (2003). Motivating struggling readers in middle school through an engagement model of classroom practice. *Reading & Writing Quarterly*, *19*(1), 59–85.

Guthrie, J.T., Wigfield, A., Humenick, N.M., Perencevich, K.C., Taboada, A., & Barbosa, P. (2006). Influences of stimulating tasks on reading motivation and comprehension. *The Journal of Educational Research*, *99*(4), 232–245.

Hakuta, K., Butler, Y.G., & Witt, D. (2000). *How long does it take English learners to attain proficiency?* (Policy Rep. 2000-1). The University of California Linguistic Minority Research Institute. Retrieved from www.eric.ed.gov/PDFS/ED443275.pdf

Haneda, M., & Wells, G. (2008). Learning an additional language through dialogic inquiry. *Language and Education*, *22*(2), 114–136.

Hansen, J. (2001). *When writers read* (2nd ed.). Portsmouth, NH: Heinemann.

Harp, S.F., & Mayer, R.E. (1997). The role of interest in learning from scientific text and illustrations: On the distinction between emotional and cognitive interest. *Journal of Educational Psychology, 89*(1), 92–102.

Harvey, S., & Goudvis, A. (2007). *Strategies that work: Teaching comprehension for understanding and engagement* (2nd ed.). Portland, ME: Stenhouse.

Heisey, N., & Kucan, L. (2010). Introducing science concepts to primary students through read-alouds: Interactions and multiple texts make the difference. *The Reading Teacher, 63*(8), 666–676.

Hickey, T.J., & DeCoste, A.E. (1998). Building bridges: Connecting high school and elementary school through short story writing. *English Journal, 88*(1), 75–78.

Hudson, R.F., Lane, H.B., & Pullen, P.C. (2005). Reading fluency assessment and instruction: What, why, and how? *The Reading Teacher, 58*(8), 702–714.

Hynd-Shanahan, C., Holschuh, J., & Hubbard, B.P. (2005). Thinking like a historian: College students' reading of multiple historical documents. *Journal of Literacy Research, 36*(2), 141–176.

Ikpeze, C.H., & Boyd, F.B. (2007). Web-based inquiry learning: Facilitating thoughtful literacy with WebQuests. *The Reading Teacher, 60*(7), 644–654.

Jalongo, M.R. (2006). *Early childhood language arts* (4th ed.). Boston, MA: Allyn & Bacon.

Johnston, P.H. (2004). *Choice words: How our language affects children's learning.* Portland, ME: Stenhouse.

Jones, R.C., & Thomas, T.G. (2006). Leave no discipline behind. *The Reading Teacher, 60*(1), 58–64.

Kamberelis, G. (1999). Genre development and learning: Children writing stories, science reports, and poems, *Research in the Teaching of English, 33*(4), 403–460.

Kame'enui, E.J., & Simmons, D.C. (2001). Introduction to this special issue: The DNA of reading fluency. *Scientific Studies of Reading, 5*(3), 203–210.

Kindler, A.L (2002). *Survey of the states' limited English proficient students and available educational programs and services: 2000–2001 summary report.* Washington, DC: National Clearinghouse for English Language Acquisition & Language Educational Programs.

Kleiner, A., & Farris, E. (2002). *Internet access in U.S. public schools and classrooms: 1994–2001* (NCES 2002-018). Washington, DC: National Center for Education Statistics, Institute of Education Sciences, U.S. Department of Education. Retrieved from www.nces.ed.gov/pubsearch/pubsinfo.asp?pubid=2002018

Knipper, K.J., & Duggan, T.J. (2006). Writing to learn across the curriculum: Tools for comprehension in content area classes. *The Reading Teacher, 59*(5), 462–470.

Kong, A., & Pearson, P.D. (2003). The road to participation: The construction of a literacy practice in a learning community of linguistically diverse learners. *Research in the Teaching of English, 38*(1), 85–124.

Kress, G. (1997). Visual and verbal modes of representation in electronically mediated communication: The potentials of new forms of text. In I. Snyder (Ed.), *Page to screen: Taking literacy into the electronic era* (pp. 55–79). Sydney, NSW, Australia: Allen & Unwin.

Kristeva, J. (1984). *Revolution in poetic language.* New York, NY: Columbia University Press.

Lehr, F., Osborn, J., & Hiebert, E.H. (2004). *Research-based practices in early reading series: A focus on vocabulary.* Retrieved from www.eric.ed.gov/PDFS/ED483190.pdf

Lenters, K. (2004). No half measures: Reading instruction for young second-language learners. *The Reading Teacher, 58*(4), 328–336.

Leu, D.J., Jr. (2000). Literacy and technology: Deictic consequences for literacy education in an information age. In M.L. Kamil, P.B. Mosenthal, P.D. Pearson, & R. Barr (Eds.), *Handbook of reading research* (Vol. 3, pp. 743–770). Mahwah, NJ: Erlbaum.

Leu, D.J., Jr., Kinzer, C.K., Coiro, J., & Cammack, D. (2004). Toward a theory of new literacies emerging from the Internet and other information and communication technologies. In R. Ruddell & Norman Unrau (Eds.), *Theoretical models and processes of reading* (5th ed., pp. 1570–1613). Newark, DE: International Reading Association.

Liu, Z. (2005). Reading behavior in the digital environment: Changes in reading behavior over the past ten years. *Journal of Documentation, 61*(6), 700–712.

Lloyd, S.L. (2004). Using comprehension strategies as a springboard for student talk. *Journal of Adolescent & Adult Literacy, 48*(2), 114–124.

MacDonald, C., & Figueredo, L. (2010). Closing the gap early: Implementing a literacy intervention for at-risk kindergartners in urban schools. *The Reading Teacher, 63*(5), 404–419.

Maloch, B., Hoffman, J.V., & Patterson, E.U. (2004). Local texts: Reading and writing "of the classroom." In J.V. Hoffman & D.L. Schallert (Eds.), *The texts in elementary classrooms* (pp. 129–138), Mahwah, NJ: Erlbaum.

Martinez, M., Roser, N.L., & Strecker, S. (1999). "I never thought I could be a star": A reader's theatre ticket to reading fluency. *The Reading Teacher, 52*(4), 326–334.

McConnell, S. (1993). Talking drawings: A strategy for assisting learners. *Journal of Reading, 36*(4), 260–269.

McKeown, M.G., & Beck, I.L. (2006). Encouraging young children's language interactions with stories. In D.K. Dickinson & S.B. Neuman (Eds.), *Handbook of early literacy research* (Vol. 2, pp. 281–294). New York, NY: Guilford.

McPherson, K. (2007). New online technologies for new literacy instruction. *Teacher Librarian, 34*(3), 69–71.

Miller, R.G., & Calfee, R.C. (2004). Making thinking visible: A method to encourage science writing in upper elementary grades. *Science and Children, 42*(3), 20–25.

Morphy, P., & Graham, S. (2012). Word processing programs and weaker writers/readers: A meta-analysis of research findings. *Reading and Writing: An Interdisciplinary Journal, 25*(3), 641–678.

Morrow, L.M., Kuhn, M.R., & Schwanenflugel, P.J. (2006). The family fluency program. *The Reading Teacher, 60*(4), 322–333.

Moss, B. (2005). Making a case and a place for effective content area literacy instruction in the elementary grades. *The Reading Teacher, 59*(1), 46–55.

Nagy, W.E., & Scott, J.A. (2000). Vocabulary processes. In M.L. Kamil, P.B. Mosenthal, P.D. Pearson, & S. Barr (Eds.), *Handbook on reading research* (Vol. 3, pp. 269–284). Mahwah, NJ: Erlbaum.

National Center for Education Statistics. (2006). *The condition of education 2006.* (NCES 2006-071). Washington, DC: U.S. Government Printing Office. Retrieved from nces.ed.gov/pubsearch/pubsinfo.asp?pubid=2006071

National Commission on Writing (2003). *The neglected "R."* New York, NY: College Entrance Examination Board.

Nesbit, C.R., Hargrove, T.Y., Harrelson, L., & Maxey, B. (2004). Implementing science notebooks in the primary grades. *Science Activities*, *40*(4). 21–29.

Nichols, M. (2006). *Comprehension through conversation: The power of purposeful talk in the reading workshop*. Portsmouth, NH: Heinemann.

Nichols, W.D., Rupley, W.H., Rickelman, R.J., & Algozzine, B. (2004). Examining phonemic awareness and concepts of print patterns of kindergarten students. *Reading Research and Instruction*, *43*(3), 56–82.

Nielsen, D.C., & Monson, D.L. (1996). Effects of literacy environment on literacy development of kindergarten children. *The Journal of Educational Research*, *89*(5), 259–271.

Ogle, D., & Blachowicz, C.L.Z. (2001). Beyond literature circles: Helping students comprehend informational texts. In C.C. Block & M. Pressley (Eds.), *Comprehension instruction: Research-based best practices* (pp. 259–274). New York, NY: Guilford.

Ogle, D., & Correa-Kovtun, A. (2010). Supporting English-language learners and struggling readers in content literacy with the "partner reading and content, too" routine. *The Reading Teacher*, *63*(7), 532–542.

Ogle, D., Klemp, R.M., & McBride, B. (2007). *Building literacy in social studies: Strategies for improving comprehension and critical thinking*. Alexandria, VA: Association for Supervision and Curriculum Development.

Otero, J. (2002). Noticing and fixing difficulties while understanding science texts. In J. Otero, J.A. Leo'n, & A.C. Graesser (Eds.), *The psychology of science text comprehension* (pp. 281–307). Mahwah, NJ: Erlbaum.

Padak, N., Newton, E., Rasinski, T., & Newton, R.M. (2008). Getting to the root of word study: Teaching Latin and Greek word roots in elementary and middle grades. In A.E. Farstrup & S.J. Samuels (Eds.), *What research has to say about vocabulary instruction* (pp. 6–31). Newark, DE: International Reading Association.

Pappas, C.C. (1993). Is narrative "primary"? Some insights from kindergarteners' pretend readings of stories and information books. *Journal of Reading Behavior*, *25*(1), 97–129.

Pappas, C.C. (2006). The information book genre: Its role in integrated science literacy research and practice. *Reading Research Quarterly*, *41*(2), 226–250.

Paratore, J. (2011). Meeting common core standards—Preparing students to read, understand, and respond to complex text [Webinar]. Retrieved from www.brainshark.com/pearsonschool/Paratore

Patall, E.A., Cooper, H., & Wynn, S.R. (2010). The effectiveness and relative importance of choice in the classroom. *Journal of Educational Psychology*, *102*(4), 896–915.

Pearson, P.D., & Gallagher, M.C. (1983). The instruction of reading comprehension. *Contemporary Educational Psychology*, *8*(3), 317–344.

Pentimonti, J.M., Zucker, T.A., Justice, L.M., & Kaderavek, J.N. (2010). Informational text use in preschool classroom read-alouds. *The Reading Teacher*, *63*(8), 656–665.

Peregoy, S.F., & Boyle, O.F. (2001). *Reading, writing, and learning in ESL: A resource book for K–12 teachers*. New York, NY: Longman.

Persky, H., Daane, M.C., & Jin, Y. (2003). *The nation's report card: Writing 2002*. Washington, DC: U.S. Department of Education Institute of Education Sciences. National Center for Education Statistics.

Piazza, C.L., & Siebert, C.F. (2008). Development and validation of a writing dispositions scale for elementary and middle school students. *The Journal of Educational Research*, *101*(5), 275–285.

Prensky, M. (2005). Listen to the natives. *Educational Leadership, 63*(4), 8–13.

Price, L.H., van Kleeck, A., & Huberty, C.J. (2009). Talk during book sharing between parents and preschool *children*: A comparison between storybook and expository book conditions. *Reading Research Quarterly, 44*(2), 171–194.

Purcell-Gates, V. (2002). Multiple literacies. In B.J. Guzzetti (Ed.), *Literacy in America: An encyclopedia of history, theory and practice* (pp. 376–380). Santa Barbara, CA: ABC CLIO.

Rasinski, T. (2006). Reading fluency instruction: Moving beyond accuracy, automaticity, and prosody. *The Reading Teacher, 59*(7), 704–706.

Rasinski, T., Padak, N., Newton, R.M., & Newton, E. (2007). *Building vocabulary from word roots*. Huntington Beach, CA: Teacher Created Materials.

Read, S. (2005). First and second graders writing informational text. *The Reading Teacher, 59*(1), 36–44.

Reutzel, D.R., Smith, J.A., & Fawson, P.C. (2005). An evaluation of two approaches for teaching reading comprehension strategies in the primary years using science informational texts. *Early Childhood Research Quarterly, 20*(3), 276–305.

Reynolds, P.L., & Symons, S. (2001). Motivational variables and children's text search. *Journal of Educational Psychology, 93*(1), 14–23.

Rice, D.C. (2002). Using trade books in teaching elementary science: Facts and fallacies. *The Reading Teacher, 55*(6), 552–565.

Risley, T. (2003, May). *Meaningful differences in the everyday experiences of young American children*. Paper presented at the annual convention of the International Reading Association, Orlando, FL.

Rosenblatt, L.M. (1938). *Literature as exploration*. New York: Appleton-Century Crofts.

Routman, R. (2003). *Reading essentials*. Portsmouth, NH: Heinemann.

Sandora, C., Beck, I., & McKeown, M. (1999). A comparison of two discussion strategies on students' comprehension and interpretation of complex literature. *Reading Psychology, 20*(3), 177–212.

Saul, E.W., & Dieckman, D. (2005). Choosing and using information trade books. *Reading Research Quarterly, 40*(4), 502–513.

Schmar-Dobler, E. (2003). Reading on the Internet: The link between literacy and technology. *Journal of Adolescent & Adult Literacy, 47*(1), 80–85.

Schraw, G., Flowerday, T., & Lehman, S. (2001). Increasing situational interest in the classroom. *Educational Psychology Review, 13*(3), 211–224.

Shanahan, T. (2006). *The National Reading Panel Report: Practical advice for teachers*. Learning Point Associates, Naperville, IL.

Shanahan, T., & Barr, R. (1995). Reading recovery: An independent evaluation of the effects of an early instructional intervention for at-risk learners. *Reading Research Quarterly, 30*(4), 958–996.

Shanahan, T., & Beck, I.L. (2006). Effective literacy teaching for English-language learners. In D. August & T. Shanahan (Eds.), *Developing literacy in second-language learners: Report of the National Literacy Panel on language-minority children and youth* (pp. 415–488). Mahwah, NJ: Erlbaum.

Shanahan, T., Fisher, D., & Frey, N. (2012). The challenge of challenging text. *Educational Leadership, 69*(6), 58–63.

Shanahan, T., & Shanahan, C. (2008). Teaching disciplinary literacy to adolescents: Rethinking content-area literacy. *Harvard Educational Review, 78*(1), 40–59.

Siegel, M. (2006). Rereading the signs: Multimodal transformation in the field of literacy education. *Language Arts, 84*(1), 65–77.

Silva, C., Weinburgh, M., Smith, K.H., Barreto, G., & Gabel, J. (2008). Partnering to develop academic language for English language learners through mathematics and science. *Childhood Education, 85*(2), 107–112.

Smith, K.P. (2001). Acknowledging, citing, going beyond: Issues of documentation in nonfiction literature. In M. Zarnowski, R.M. Kerper, & J.M. Jensen (Eds.), *The best in children's nonfiction: Reading, writing, and teaching Orbis Pictus Award books* (pp. 32–41). Urbana, IL: National Council of Teachers of English.

Smith, M.C. (2000). The real-world reading practices of adults. *Journal of Literacy Research, 32*(1), 25–52.

Smolin, L.I., & Lawless, K.A. (2003). Becoming literate in the technological age: New responsibilities and tools for teachers. *The Reading Teacher, 56*(6), 570–577.

Smolkin, L.B., & Donovan, C.A. (2001). The contexts of comprehension: The information book read aloud, comprehension acquisition, and comprehension instruction in a first-grade classroom. *The Elementary School Journal, 102*(2), 97–122.

Soares, L.B., & Wood, K. (2010). A critical literacy perspective for teaching and learning social studies. *The Reading Teacher, 63*(6), 486–494.

Stahl, S.A., & Murray, B.A. (1994). Defining phonological awareness and its relationship to early reading. *Journal of Educational Psychology, 86*(2), 221–234.

Stahl, S.A., & Shanahan, C. (2004). Learning to think like a historian: Disciplinary knowledge through critical analysis of multiple documents. In T.L. Jetton & J.A. Dole (Eds.), *Adolescent literacy research and practice* (pp. 94–118). New York, NY: Guilford.

Stanovich, K.E. (1986). Matthew effects in reading: Some consequences of individual differences in the acquisition of literacy. *Reading Research Quarterly, 21*(4), 360–406.

Stanovich, K.E. (1991). Word recognition: Changing perspectives. In R. Barr, M.L. Kamil, P. Mosenthal, & P.D. Pearson (Eds.), *Handbook of reading research* (Vol. 2, pp. 418–452). New York, NY: Longman.

Sudol, P., & King, C.M. (1996). A checklist for choosing nonfiction trade books. *The Reading Teacher, 49*(5), 422–424.

Sutherland-Smith, W. (2002). Weaving the literacy web: Changes in reading from page to screen. *The Reading Teacher, 55*(7), 662–669.

Teale, W.H. (1984). Reading to young children: Its significance for literacy development. In H. Goelman, A.A. Oberg, & F. Smith (Eds.), *Awakening to literacy* (pp. 110–121). London, England: Heinemann.

Teale, W.H. (2009). Students learning English and their literacy instruction in urban schools. *The Reading Teacher, 62*(8), 699–703.

Tompkins, G. (2009). *Language arts: Patterns of practice* (7th ed.). Boston, MA: Allyn & Bacon.

Trelease, J. (2013). *The read-aloud handbook* (7th ed.). New York, NY: Penguin.

United States Department of Labor. (2000). *Learning a living: A blueprint for high-performance. A SCANS report for America 2000*. Retrieved from wdr.doleta.gov/SCANS/lal/lal.pdf

Vacca, R.T., & Vacca, J.A.L. (2008). *Content area reading: Literacy and learning across the curriculum* (9th ed.). Boston, MA: Allyn & Bacon.

VanSledright, B. (2002). Confronting history's interpretive paradox while teaching fifth graders to investigate the past. *American Educational Research Journal, 39*(4), 1089–1115.

Venezky, R.L. (2000). The origins of the present-day chasm between adult literacy needs and school literacy instruction. *Scientific Studies of Reading, 4*(1), 19–39.

Wade, S.E., Buxton, W.M., & Kelly, M. (1999). Using think-alouds to examine reader-text interest. *Reading Research Quarterly, 34*(2), 194–216.

Wagstaff, J.M. (1997). Building practical knowledge of letter-sound correspondences: A beginner's word wall and beyond. *The Reading Teacher, 51*(4), 298–304.

Webster, P.S. (2009). Exploring the literature of fact. *The Reading Teacher, 62*(8), 662–671.

White, S. (2012). Mining the text: 34 text features that can ease or obstruct text comprehension and use. *Literacy Research and Instruction, 51*(2), 143–164.

Wigfield, A., Guthrie, J.T., Tonks, S., & Perencevich, K.C. (2004). Children's motivation for reading: Domain specificity and instructional influences. *Journal of Educational Research, 97*(6), 299–309.

Williams, J.P., Stafford, K.B., Lauer, K.D., Hall, K.M., & Pollini, S. (2009). Embedding reading comprehension training in content-area instruction. *Journal of Educational Psychology, 101*(1), 1–20.

Wineburg, S., & Martin, D. (2004). Reading and rewriting history. *Educational Leadership, 62*(1), 42–45.

Wollman-Bonilla, J.E. (2001). Can first-grade writers demonstrate audience awareness? *Reading Research Quarterly, 36*(2), 184–201.

Yopp, H.K., & Yopp, R.H. (2000). Supporting phonemic awareness development in the classroom. *The Reading Teacher, 54*(2), 130–143.

Yopp, R.H., & Yopp, H.K. (2006). Informational texts as read-alouds at school and home. *Journal of Literacy Research, 38*(1), 37–51.

Yuan, T. (2011). From Ponyo to "My Garfield story": Using digital comics as an alternative pathway to literary composition. *Childhood Education, 87*(4), 297–301.

LITERATURE CITED

Barretta, G. (2010). *Dear deer: A book of homophones.* New York, NY: Square Fish.

Bishop, N. (2007). *Spiders.* New York, NY : Scholastic.

Boothroyd, J. (2012). *From chalkboards to computers: How schools have changed.* Minneapolis, MN: Lerner.

Boothroyd, J. (2012). *From marbles to video games: How toys have changed.* Minneapolis, MN: Lerner.

Boothroyd, J. (2012). *From typewriters to text messages: How communication has changed.* Minneapolis, MN: Lerner.

Brennan-Nelson, D. (2003). *My momma likes to say.* Ann Arbor, MI: Sleeping Bear.

Brennan-Nelson, D. (2004). *My teacher likes to say.* Ann Arbor, MI: Sleeping Bear.

Brennan-Nelson, D. (2007). *My grandma likes to say.* Ann Arbor, MI: Sleeping Bear.

Brennan-Nelson, D. (2009). *My daddy likes to say.* Ann Arbor, MI: Sleeping Bear.

Carney, E. (2009). *National Geographic readers: Frogs!* Washington, DC: National Geographic Society.

Cleary, B.P. (2007). *How much can a bare bear bear? What are homonyms and homophones?* Minneapolis, MN: First Avenue.

Delta Science Readers (2003). *Finding the moon.* Nashua, NH: Delta Education.

Foster, K. (2008). *Atlas of South America.* Minneapolis, MN: Picture Window.

Garrett, G. (2005). *Scientists ask questions.* New York, NY: Scholastic.

Gibbons, G. (1993). *From seed to plant.* New York, NY: Holiday House.

Gwynne, F. (1976). *A chocolate moose for dinner.* New York, NY: Prentice-Hall.

Gwynne, F. (1988). *The king who rained.* New York, NY: Aladdin.

Hoberman, M.A. (2001). *You read to me, I'll read to you: Very short stories to read together.* Boston, MA: Little, Brown.

Hoberman, M.A. (2004). *You read to me, I'll read to you: Very short fairy tales to read together.* New York, NY: Little, Brown.

Hoose, P.M., Hoose, H., & Tilley, D. (1998). *Hey, little ant.* Berkeley, CA: Tricycle.

Hudson, W. (1991). *Jamal's busy day.* East Orange, NJ: Just Us.

Komiya, T. (2008). *Life-size zoo.* Shanghai, China: Seven Footer Kids.

Larson, J.S. (2010). *What can you do with money? Earning, spending, and saving.* Minneapolis, MN: Lerner.

Leedy, L., & Street, P. (2003). *There's a frog in my throat!: 440 animal sayings a little bird told me.* New York, NY: Holiday House.

Lehn, B. (1999). *What is a scientist?* Minneapolis, MN: Millbrook.

Lobel, A. (2004). *The frog and toad collection.* New York, NY: HarperCollins.

Loewen, N. (2007). *If you were a homonym or a homophone.* Mankato, MN: Picture Window.

Mariconda, B. (2008). *Sort it out!* Mt. Pleasant, SC: Sylvan Dell.

Morgan, S. (2011). *Our senses: How sight works.* New York, NY: PowerKids.

Moses, W. (2008). *Raining cats and dogs: A collection of irresistible idioms and illustrations to tickle the funny bones of young people.* New York, NY: Philomel.

Nelson, K.L. (2010). *Monster trucks on the move.* Minneapolis, MN: Lerner.

Nelson, R. (2010). *What do we buy? A look at goods and services.* Minneapolis, MN: Lerner.

Nelson, R. (2013). *Let's make a bar graph.* Minneapolis, MN: Lerner.

Rissman, R. (2010). *The five senses: Tasting.* Chicago, IL: Heinemann Library.

Simon, S. (2003). *Eyes and ears.* New York, NY: HarperCollins.

Slepian, J., & Seidler, A. (1967/2001). *The hungry thing.* New York, NY: Scholastic.

Slepian, J., & Seidler, A. (1990/1993). *The hungry thing returns.* New York, NY: Scholastic.

Slepian, J., & Seidler, A. (1993). *The hungry thing goes to a restaurant.* New York, NY: Scholastic.

Snodgrass, C.S. (2008). *Super silly sayings that are over your head: A children's illustrated book of idioms.* Higganum, CT: Starfish Specialty.

Terban, M. (2007). *Eight ate: A feast of homonym riddles.* New York, NY: Sandpiper.

Terban, M. (2007). *In a pickle and other funny idioms.* New York, NY: Houghton Mifflin.

Wilson, K. (2007). *A frog in a bog.* New York, NY: Aladdin.

INDEX

Note. Page numbers followed by *f*, *t*, and *r* refer to figures, tables, and reproducibles, respectively.